TIME KILLS DEALS

ARE YOU THE TIME KILLER?

Book 1 of The Keys Series

By Dr. Chris Guam Santos

COPYRIGHT

Time Kills Deals: Are You the Time Killer?

ISBN: 979-8-9969533-0-1

Published by Santos Performance Group

Richmond, Virginia

First Edition, 2026

Printed in the United States of America

For bulk orders, speaking engagements, and dealership training inquiries:

www.ChrisGuamSantos.com

*The information in this book reflects the author's personal experience and professional practice. Names of specific dealerships and individuals have been omitted or changed where appropriate. Results may vary. The author and

DEDICATION

To every salesperson who ever let a deal walk out the door and spent the drive home replaying what they should have said.

This book is for you.

It is also for the managers who refuse to accept mediocrity on their floors, the trainers who still believe in the fundamentals, and the rookie who showed up on a Monday with nothing but hunger and a willingness to learn.

The two keys in this book are simple. They are not secret. They are not complicated. The only question is whether you will actually use them.

Get to work.

FOREWORD: WHY THESE TWO PRINCIPLES CHANGED EVERYTHING

I've been in automotive sales for a long time. Long enough to have worked every chair on the floor — floor salesperson, closer, finance manager, desk manager, General Sales Manager, and ultimately General Manager. I've watched thousands of customers walk through a dealership door and either drive off in a new vehicle or drive off in the same car they came in.

Here's the uncomfortable truth I learned early: the difference between those two outcomes almost never came down to price. It almost never came down to inventory. And it almost never came down to the customer's ability to buy.

It came down to the salesperson.

More specifically, it came down to whether the salesperson was *running a process* — or just having a conversation.

I've seen charming, funny, naturally gifted talkers produce mediocre numbers month after month. And I've seen quiet, methodical, process-driven professionals who you wouldn't notice at a party absolutely destroy their sales targets every single month without fail. The difference was not personality. The difference was discipline.

Two principles define great sales floors. Two principles that, once I committed to them completely, changed the way I looked at every single interaction on the lot.

The first: **Time Kills Deals.**

Not sometimes. Not usually. Always. Every minute a customer is not moving forward in the process, they are moving backward. Doubt creeps in. The internet beckons. A competitor's ad pops up on their phone. A family member who hasn't even seen the vehicle suddenly has opinions. Time is never neutral in a sales environment. It is always working against you.

The second: **Every Deal Every Time.**

This means running the same process, with the same discipline, on every single customer who walks through your door — regardless of whether they look like a buyer, regardless of whether they say they're "just looking," regardless of whether you're tired or slammed or it's 6:45 on a Saturday evening. Every deal. Every time. No exceptions.

Together, these two principles do something remarkable. They take the chaos, the unpredictability, and the emotion out of selling — and they replace it with a system. A system that works. A system that closes deals.

This book is my attempt to lay out everything I know about those two principles — where they come from, why they work, how to apply them, and why most salespeople resist them right up until the moment they stop resisting and their numbers transform.

I'm not interested in theories. I'm not interested in academic models or fancy frameworks with acronyms that won't survive contact with an actual customer.

What you'll find in these pages is what works on an actual sales floor with actual human beings who walked in because they need transportation and they're nervous about money and they've already spent two hours reading reviews online.

These are not new ideas. But they are still the right ideas. And in most dealerships, on most floors, they are being ignored every single day.

That ends here.

Let's get to work.

— Dr. Chris Guam Santos

INTRODUCTION: THE TWO KEYS THAT RUN EVERY GREAT SALES FLOOR

Walk into any top-performing dealership in the country — doesn't matter the brand, doesn't matter the city — and you'll find the same thing underneath all the different styles, personalities, and inventory mixes.

You'll find urgency and you'll find process.

That's it. That's the formula.

The top performers on those floors are not all outgoing. They're not all former athletes or natural born closers who can talk anyone into anything. Some are quiet. Some are analytical. Some are women, some are men, some have been doing this for thirty years and some are in their first year. What they all share is a relentless commitment to moving the deal forward — every minute, every interaction — and a locked-in discipline around running the same process on every customer, every time.

That is what this book is about.

The Problem Most Sales Floors Have Right Now

Most dealerships have decent training materials sitting in a binder somewhere. Most sales managers can recite the Road to the Sale in their sleep. Most salespeople have heard the basics of how a deal is supposed to flow from greeting to delivery.

And yet deals die every single day on those floors.

They die because a salesperson spent twenty minutes in small talk and never moved toward the desk. They die because nobody asked for the trade payoff until it was too late and the customer felt ambushed. They die because the write-up sheet sat blank on the manager's desk when the customer walked out saying they wanted to "think about it." They die because a salesperson decided the customer wasn't serious and gave them their space — and the customer drove two miles down the road and bought from a competitor.

Deals don't die because the market is bad. Deals don't die because inventory is limited or rates are high or the customer was impossible. Deals die because someone didn't run the process. Someone let time pass without moving forward. Someone chose comfort over commitment.

This book is the answer to that problem.

What You're Going to Learn

We're going to cover everything — from the psychology of urgency to the exact word tracks you should use when a customer says they want to think about it. We're going to tear apart the write-up sheet and show you why it is the single most powerful closing tool on your floor. We're going to talk about why salespeople resist the process, what that resistance is really costing them, and how to overcome it.

We're going to talk about real buyers and tire kickers and how to tell the difference in under five minutes.

We're going to give managers the tools to build a culture of process discipline from the top down. And we're going to show you how every single principle in this book translates directly to real estate, insurance, financial services, home improvement, and any other high-ticket sales environment.

We'll end with a 30-day action plan you can start tomorrow.

One Warning

These principles only work if you use them. Knowledge sitting on a shelf doesn't close deals. A word track you memorized but never deploy doesn't close deals. A process you understand intellectually but don't actually run doesn't close deals.

The salespeople who will get the most out of this book are the ones who are willing to feel slightly uncomfortable for a few weeks while they build new habits. The ones who are willing to ask for the driver's license when it feels early. The ones who are willing to guide the customer to the desk when the customer wants to keep walking the lot. The ones who are willing to be a professional, not just a nice person.

That's the one requirement for this book to work: you have to be willing to do what it says.

Everything else is just information.

Two keys. Zero excuses.

Let's go.

PART ONE: THE ENEMY IS TIME

CHAPTER 1: TIME IS THE ENEMY

Here is a fact about human decision-making that most salespeople never fully internalize, even though it explains almost everything about why deals close or fall apart.

Emotion drives purchase decisions. Logic kills them.

When a customer walks onto your lot, they are almost always running on emotion. They're excited about a new car. They're tired of their current payment. They have a growing family and the sedan isn't cutting it anymore. Their lease is up and they've already been looking online for three weeks. Somewhere in their gut, they've already made a decision. They want a new vehicle.

Your job — at its most basic level — is to keep that emotional momentum going forward until it culminates in a purchase.

Time is your enemy in that mission. Because time doesn't freeze the emotional state. Time drains it.

The Emotional Cooling Effect

Think of a customer's excitement and buying energy as a cup of hot coffee. It's hot when they arrive. It stays hot while things are moving — when they're looking at vehicles, sitting in the driver's seat, talking about features, imagining themselves in the car. But the moment things stop moving — the moment there's a long pause, an awkward silence, a wait while you go "check on something" — that coffee starts to cool.

And once it cools enough, the customer's rational brain takes over.

The rational brain says: *Do I really need this right now? Maybe I should wait. Maybe I should check online first. Maybe I should ask my sister who knows about cars. This is a lot of money.*

That's the moment you've lost them. Not because the deal was bad. Not because the car was wrong. Because time did what time always does — it let doubt in.

Here's what every experienced dealership manager will tell you: the customer who says "I want to think about it" almost never comes back. Studies of dealership traffic consistently show that customers who leave without buying return at rates well below 20 percent. Most of those who "just need to think about it" go home, get on their phone, and buy from another dealer within 48 hours.

They didn't need more time to decide. They needed someone to guide them to a decision.

The Competitor in Your Customer's Pocket

In 1985, when a customer left a dealership to "think about it," they went home. Maybe they called another dealership. Maybe they looked in the newspaper. The competitive landscape was limited.

Today, that customer leaves your lot and within sixty seconds has:

- Three competing dealers' inventory on their screen
- A price comparison tool
- A payment calculator
- Five Reddit threads arguing about whether your brand is worth it
- A cousin who texted back "honestly just wait, end of month deals are better"

The internet is a deal-killing machine when you let it become the next step in the process. Time doesn't just give doubt room to grow — it gives your competitors direct access to your customer.

Every hour that passes after a customer leaves without buying is an hour your competition has them. Not hypothetically. Literally. Retargeting ads, Google searches, AutoTrader notifications — the moment they leave your lot and start browsing, they are being marketed to by everyone who is not you.

Speed is not just good manners. Speed is competitive strategy.

The "They'll Come Back" Lie

Let's talk about the most comfortable lie in sales: *"They said they'll come back this weekend."*

Some customers mean it when they say it. Most don't. Not because they're dishonest — but because something will happen between now and the weekend that changes things. Life intervenes. The emotion cools. A different car catches their eye. Their spouse raises a concern. They find a slightly better deal somewhere else.

The salesperson who says "they'll come back" is often protecting themselves from the discomfort of a hard conversation right now. It feels less confrontational to let them go with a smile and an expectation that they'll return than to say "before you leave, let me show you what the numbers actually look like."

Here's the truth: if you don't do everything in your power to close the deal today, you are leaving the outcome to chance. You are betting your commission check — and your customer's transportation needs —

on the hope that nothing will derail the deal between now and Saturday.

That is not selling. That is hoping.

Real Stories From the Floor

Every seasoned salesperson has a version of this story:

A customer comes in on a Tuesday evening, about an hour before close. They've been researching a specific model for weeks. They love it. They sit in it. Their eyes light up. They talk about where they're going to take it on their first road trip. The salesperson is tired, it's late, and the customer says they want to bring their spouse by on the weekend.

The salesperson says, "Absolutely, we'll see you Saturday."

Saturday comes. The customer doesn't show. A call goes unanswered. Two weeks later, the salesperson spots the same model — different color — driving past the dealership. It's the customer. They bought from someone else.

What happened? The Tuesday-night salesperson gave the customer time. Time to go home and show their spouse pictures. Time for the spouse to say "did you ask about the trade?" Time for both of them to go to a different dealer on Friday just to "compare." Time for a different salesperson — one who didn't give them time — to close the deal.

That Tuesday-night salesperson did everything right except one thing: they didn't run the process right then, right there, with everything they had.

Here is another one:

A couple walks in on a Saturday morning. They're trading in their vehicle, they have a rough idea of what they want for payments, and they're motivated — they're moving across state in three weeks and need a reliable car. They spend forty-five minutes with a salesperson walking the lot, test driving, and talking about features.

Then the salesperson says, "Let me go grab my manager and see what we can do on your trade."

Twenty minutes pass. The salesperson is at the desk, talking to the manager, trying to get a number. Nobody goes back to the customers. They're sitting in the showroom. The coffee is cooling. One pulls out their phone. The other looks at their watch.

When the salesperson comes back, the couple is polite but something has shifted. They want to "come back after lunch." They don't.

What killed that deal? Twenty minutes of dead air. Twenty minutes of the customer sitting with their thoughts, their doubt, and their smartphone.

Urgency is not about being pushy. Urgency is about respecting the customer's emotional momentum and refusing to let it die on your floor.

The 10-Minute Rule

Here is a practical standard every salesperson should internalize: **No customer should ever go more than ten minutes without a meaningful interaction.**

That doesn't mean pestering them. It means checking in, moving to the next step, answering a question they haven't thought to ask yet, or inviting them to take the next action. It means you are always, actively, moving the deal forward.

The salesperson who says "I just wanted to give them some space" while their customer stews in the showroom for twenty minutes is not being respectful. They are being negligent. They are letting the deal die in slow motion.

Movement closes deals. Stillness kills them.

The Compound Effect of Delay

Here's the thing most salespeople don't think about: urgency compounds. Every minute of movement creates more momentum. Every pause creates more friction.

Think of the deal as a boulder rolling downhill. When it's moving, physics is on your side — it gets easier to keep rolling. But the moment it stops, you have to break static friction all over again to get it moving. And every time you stop and restart, the customer has to re-commit emotionally. Every re-commitment is a chance for them to commit the other way.

Keep it moving. Always keep it moving.

BOTTOM LINE: Your customer's buying energy is finite and perishable. Every minute of delay — intentional or not — bleeds that energy away. Your competitors are waiting for the moment your customer stops moving forward. Don't give them the opening.

TAKEAWAYS:

- Buying decisions are emotional. Logic and time kill them.
- Customers who leave without buying rarely return — well under 20% come back.
- The internet gives your competitors direct access to your customer the moment they leave your lot.
- "They'll come back" is the comfortable lie that costs you your commission.
- No more than ten minutes should pass without a meaningful, forward-moving interaction.

CHAPTER 2: ARE YOU THE TIME KILLER?

Here is the uncomfortable question nobody on the sales floor wants to answer honestly:

Who is killing your deals?

Most salespeople, if pressed, will point somewhere external. The economy. The rates. The inventory. The customer who "wasn't really serious." The competitor down the road who is apparently selling cars for nothing.

The real answer, in most cases, is a lot closer to home.

The most dangerous person to your deal might be you.

This is not said to be cruel. It is said because it is true and because recognizing it is the first step to changing it. The salesperson who understands exactly how they are killing their own deals has the power to stop. The salesperson who blames external factors never does.

Let's walk through the seven ways salespeople kill their own deals. Be honest as you read. If you recognize yourself in more than two of these, you have significant room to grow — and significant upside waiting for you if you do the work.

1. The Small Talk Trap

Small talk is fine. It builds rapport. A little "how's your day going, where are you coming from" is completely appropriate in the first sixty seconds of an interaction.

The trap is when small talk becomes the entire interaction.

There are salespeople who are genuinely excellent conversationalists. Funny. Warm. Likeable. Customers love being around them. And those same salespeople will sometimes go twenty, thirty, forty minutes deep into a customer interaction — talking about sports, kids, the weather, vacation plans — without ever actually moving toward a deal.

At the end of that conversation, the customer loves the salesperson and feels no particular urgency to buy anything. They feel like they've just visited with a friend. And friends don't usually pressure you to make a major financial decision.

Small talk is the opening act. It is not the show.

Key: After no more than two to three minutes of rapport-building, begin transitioning to needs assessment. The customer did not drive to a dealership to make a new friend — they came because they need a vehicle.

2. The "I'll Give Them Space" Myth

This one comes from a good place. Salespeople who have been on the customer's side of the equation remember how annoying it is to be followed around. They want to be different. They want to be the low-pressure dealership experience.

So they back off. They let the customer wander. They watch from a respectful distance and wait to be called upon.

This approach has two fatal problems.

First: the customer is now without a guide in an environment full of choices and information they don't know how to process. That is not respectful — it is abandonment. Your job is to help them make a decision. You cannot help from twenty feet away.

Second: while you're giving them space, their brain is filling that space. With questions. With doubts. With a desire to go research something on their phone before committing. With the memory of their brother-in-law saying "never make a decision the first day."

Giving space feels polite. What it actually does is give doubt a place to live.

The professional approach: Stay close enough to engage, stay available, and move the process forward every few minutes. This is called being present, not pushy.

3. The Information Dump

This one is more common among newer salespeople and those who have product knowledge they're proud of. They launch into every feature, every spec, every option available, in a rapid-fire monologue that leaves the customer glazed over.

The customer came in with a problem — they need transportation. They did not come in for a lecture on the 8-speed transmission and all-wheel-drive torque distribution.

When you spend fifteen minutes talking about features the customer didn't ask about, two things happen: you lose them emotionally (nobody wants to be talked at), and you delay the move toward the desk and the numbers.

The information dump feels like expertise. It functions as a stall.

Key: Discuss the features that solve the customer's specific problem. Then move forward.

4. The Price Avoider

Some salespeople are terrified of talking about money. They will walk the lot, do the demo, sit in the vehicle, drive the route — and do everything they possibly can to avoid the moment when numbers have to come out.

Usually this comes from a fear of the customer's reaction. If we talk about money, they might balk. They might say it's too expensive. They might get upset. So as long as we don't talk about money, we haven't been rejected.

Here is the thing: you work at a dealership. Everyone knows that at some point, a number is going to come up. Avoiding that moment doesn't make it go away — it just pushes it to a point where both parties are more emotionally invested and therefore more likely to blow up when the number feels different than expected.

The price avoider is not protecting the customer. They're protecting themselves. And every minute they avoid the financial conversation is a minute spent building emotional investment in a deal that hasn't even been started yet.

The professional move: Get to the numbers early. Not aggressively — through the worksheet. Through process. "Let's put everything on one sheet and see if the numbers work for you." Early and calm beats late and emotional every time.

5. The "Be Back" Enabler

You know this one. The customer starts drifting toward the door. They say they want to think about it. They say they'll be back.

And the salesperson, rather than trying to understand what's really going on, opens the door for them. "Of course, take your time, here's my card."

This salesperson has just abdicated their entire role in the sales process. They have handed the decision to the customer — someone who is not a sales professional, who is emotionally ambiguous, who is about to go get back in their car and leave. They have essentially said: "I trust you to make this decision without my help. Good luck."

The "be back" enabler isn't being respectful. They're being a quitter.

The professional response to "I want to think about it" is not compliance — it's curiosity. "I completely understand. What part of this would you like to think about? Is it the payment, the trade, the model itself?" You're not arguing. You're not begging. You're doing your job: figuring out what's in the way and seeing if you can address it.

6. The Assumption Merchant

This salesperson has already decided, based on how the customer looks or what they're driving or what they say in the first two minutes, exactly how this interaction is going to go. They've looked at the trade, estimated the equity, and already decided in their head that this doesn't work. Or they've decided the customer isn't serious based on no actual information whatsoever.

The assumption merchant does not run the full process because they have already mentally checked out of the deal.

This is one of the most expensive habits in sales. You will be wrong about customers constantly. The person in worn-out jeans and an old car might have outstanding credit and cash in the bank. The person who says "I'm just looking" might buy today if someone guides them properly. The customer who seems difficult might become your easiest deal if someone actually tries.

Never decide a deal is dead before the process has told you it's dead. The process is how you find out what's actually possible. Your assumptions are just guesses.

7. The "Let Me Know If You Have Any Questions" Offender

Save the worst for last.

This sentence — "let me know if you have any questions" — is the single lowest-performing sentence in automotive sales. It is the white flag of the sales interaction. It signals that you have completely surrendered control of the process and transferred all responsibility to the customer.

Think about what you're actually saying: *I have no idea what to do next, so I'm going to make you responsible for advancing this interaction. Good luck figuring out what question to ask.*

Customers who don't know what to ask don't ask anything. They leave.

Every interaction should end with you directing the next step. Not "let me know if you have any questions." Instead: "Let me show you what this one looks like on the inside." "Let's take it around the block real quick." "Why don't we sit down and put the numbers together so you can see what this actually looks like for you." You always have a next step. Always.

The Self-Assessment: Are You a Time Killer?

Answer honestly. Score yourself on a scale of 1–5 (1 = never, 5 = all the time):

1. I spend more than three minutes in small talk before moving to needs assessment. ___

2. I back away from customers to give them "space" instead of staying engaged. ___

3. I give extended feature explanations customers didn't ask for. ___

4. I avoid talking about money for as long as possible. ___

5. When a customer moves toward the door, I facilitate their exit rather than engage the real objection. ___

6. I have already decided a deal won't work before the process has confirmed it. ___

7. I use the phrase "let me know if you have any questions." ___

Total: ___/35

Scoring:

- 7–14: You are process-disciplined. Focus on tightening the edges.
- 15–21: You have identifiable habits that are costing you deals. Pick the highest score and eliminate it this week.

- 22–28: Significant opportunity to improve. This book will show you exactly how.
- 29–35: You are currently your own biggest obstacle. Commit fully to what follows and your numbers will change dramatically.

BOTTOM LINE: The deals you're losing aren't all being lost to the market or the competition. Many of them are being lost in the thirty-second decisions you make in the course of every customer interaction. Identify your time-killing habits. Eliminate them.

TAKEAWAYS:

- Small talk builds rapport; it is never the process.
- Giving customers "space" hands them over to their doubts.
- Avoiding the money conversation protects you, not the customer.
- "Let me know if you have any questions" is the white flag of professional sales.
- Never pre-judge a deal before the process has run.

CHAPTER 3: THE MYTH OF THE EASY SALE

Every salesperson has experienced it. The customer who walks in already knowing exactly what they want, already pre-approved, already done their research, already mentally bought. They pick the vehicle. They barely flinch at the number. They sign quickly. They're gone in two hours and you made a great commission with almost no effort.

These customers exist. They are real. They are also the single most dangerous thing that can happen to a developing salesperson.

Because that easy deal teaches exactly the wrong lessons.

What the Easy Deal Teaches You (That Isn't True)

The easy deal teaches you that sales is primarily about matching customers to products. The customer knows what they want, you show it to them, the numbers work, everybody's happy.

The easy deal teaches you that customers who seem hesitant or difficult are probably not real buyers — because your easy customers were never hesitant or difficult.

The easy deal teaches you that if you just make yourself available and pleasant and low-pressure, the right customers will find you and transact with you without much friction.

Every single one of these lessons is wrong.

The Comfortable Path to Mediocrity

A salesperson who survives primarily on easy deals never builds the skills required to close a hard deal. And the hard deals — the customers who are hesitant, who say they're just looking, who have trade issues, who have credit issues, who have spouses who weren't there for the first visit — those are where the real money is.

Here's the math: easy deals represent maybe 10–15% of your potential customer base on any given month. If you're only closing easy deals, you are leaving 85% of your opportunity on the table.

The salespeople who are consistently at the top of the board — month after month, not just in good markets — are the ones who can close the hard ones. And you don't learn to close the hard ones by waiting for the easy ones.

Real skill is built in the friction.

The "They'll Come Back" Fantasy, Revisited

The myth of the easy sale has a close cousin: the belief that good customers naturally come back when they're ready.

This is the passive salesperson's religion. *I'll plant good seeds. I'll be friendly. I'll create a great experience. And the right people will return when they're ready to buy.*

This philosophy produces one specific career outcome: the salesperson who has been at the same dealership for eight years, is genuinely liked by everyone, and produces numbers just good enough to not be fired.

They are surviving on relationship-driven repeat business and the occasional walk-in who was already sold before they arrived. They have never learned to convert a skeptical customer. They have never developed the process muscles required to take a "I'm just looking" and turn it into a signature.

They are comfortable. And they are underperforming.

Hard Conversations Are Where Deals Live

The customer who says they're just looking — that's a deal waiting to happen if you handle the next five minutes correctly.

The customer who asks "what's your best price?" before they've even sat down — that's a customer who is engaged, interested, and using language they learned from the internet because nobody has ever shown them a better way to have this conversation.

The customer who wants to think about it — that's almost always a customer who has a specific concern they haven't yet felt safe voicing. Find the concern. Address it. Close the deal.

None of these conversations are easy. All of them are winnable.

But you can't win them if you've spent your career avoiding friction. You have to have been through the hard conversations enough times that they stop feeling hard. That only comes from doing them, repeatedly, even when it's uncomfortable, even when the customer seems annoyed, even when the easy move is to back off and say "let me know if you have any questions."

The Student vs. The Comfortable

There are two types of salespeople when it comes to difficult customers.

The first type says: *This one's going to be a problem. Let me not invest too much energy here.*

The second type says: *This is a training rep. I'm going to run the full process on this customer and see what happens.*

The first type stays average. The second type gets better every day.

Here's the thing about difficult customers: they cannot hurt you. The worst outcome is they leave without buying. That was always a possible outcome. But if you run the process correctly on a difficult customer and close them, you have just developed a skill you will have forever. The rep was worth far more than the commission.

What to Do With an Easy Customer

None of this means you should make easy customers difficult. When the easy deal comes, take it. Be grateful. Deliver an excellent experience.

But do not let the easy deal become your standard. Do not let it convince you that you're good at sales when what you're actually good at is transacting with pre-decided customers.

Use every easy deal as a reminder that there are hard deals waiting right behind it — and that the only way to grow is to go after them with the same process, the same intensity, and the same commitment.

Because here's the truth: **every top performer on every great sales floor got there by closing the deals everyone else gave up on.**

The deals they didn't think were winnable. The customer who said no twice. The trade situation that looked upside down at first glance. The credit profile that seemed impossible until someone ran the process all the way through and found a path.

Those are the deals that build careers. Not the easy ones.

BOTTOM LINE: Easy deals don't make great salespeople. They make comfortable ones. The skills that separate the top 10% from everyone else are built in hard conversations, difficult customers, and deals that require real process. Go after the hard ones.

TAKEAWAYS:

- Easy deals teach the wrong lessons about what selling actually is.
- Relying on walk-in buyers and repeat customers produces average results at best.
- Hard conversations are winnable if you have a process.
- Every difficult customer is a training rep that makes you permanently better.
- The top performers on any floor built their careers on closing deals others gave up on.

CHAPTER 4: PROCESS IS POWER

Let's talk about something that separates great dealerships from average ones, great salespeople from average ones, and great closers from people who just talk to customers.

Process.

Not personality. Not charm. Not a "gift" for sales. Process.

Walk into the top-performing dealerships in your region — the ones consistently in the upper percentile for volume and CSI — and you will find something consistent: everyone on the floor is running the same process. Not the exact same conversation — people have different styles, different energies, different relationships with customers. But underneath those personalities, there is a structure. A sequence. A flow that every deal goes through from the moment someone drives on the lot to the moment they drive off in a new vehicle.

That structure is what closes deals. Not the personality on top of it.

The Road to the Sale

Most salespeople have heard this term. Fewer actually use it as a serious framework. Let's be clear about what it is and why it matters.

The Road to the Sale is not a checklist created by corporate training departments to give new hires something to memorize. It is a sequenced process developed through decades of studying what actually happens in successful automotive transactions — and building that sequence into a repeatable system.

The stages, broadly, are:

8. **Meet and Greet** — First contact, rapport establishment.

9. **Needs Assessment** — Understanding what the customer actually needs, not just what they think they want.

10. **Vehicle Selection** — Matching the right product to the identified need.

11. **Product Presentation / Demo Drive** — Building emotional investment in the specific vehicle.

12. **Write-Up / Needs Assessment Sheet** — The Every Deal Every Time sheet. The anchor of this entire book.

13. **Desk** — Working the numbers with management.

14. **Close** — Agreement on terms.

15. **F&I** — Finance and insurance, protecting the deal and the customer.

16. **Delivery** — Completing the process, beginning the relationship.

Every step has a purpose. Every step moves the customer forward in a specific, deliberate way. Skip a step, or rush through it carelessly, and the step after it becomes harder. Blow through the needs assessment to get to the demo faster, and you end up demoing the wrong vehicle. Skip the write-up and go straight to negotiating on price, and you lose control of the entire conversation.

Why Process Beats Personality

Here's the dangerous myth: the best salespeople are the ones who are naturally good with people. The charming ones. The ones who can walk up to anyone and build rapport in sixty seconds.

Personality matters. I'm not dismissing it. But personality without process is just entertainment. And entertainment doesn't close deals.

Think about it this way: a naturally charming salesperson who does not run a consistent process will have volatile months. They'll crush it in October when the right customers happen to come through the door, and they'll struggle in December when the floor traffic is tougher. Their success depends on things outside their control — who walks in, what mood those customers are in, whether the market is moving.

A process-disciplined salesperson has a floor. Their worst month is still competitive because they're running the process on every single customer, extracting every possible deal from the available traffic, and not letting anything slip through because of laziness or comfort.

You want a career in sales? Build your floor. Learn the process. Master it so completely that it runs automatically even when you're tired, even when it's been a slow day, even when the customer in front of you looks like they're not buying anything.

Process Is What Separates the Professional from the Amateur

Here's a question: what's the difference between a doctor and someone who has read a lot of WebMD?

One of them runs a process. Every time. Regardless of the patient. The intake questions. The examination. The diagnosis. The treatment plan. The follow-up. They don't skip the process because a patient walks in saying they already know what's wrong with them. They don't skip the examination because the patient seems healthy. They run the process, every time, because the process is what produces accurate outcomes.

A salesperson who doesn't run the process is not a professional. They're a friendly person with some product knowledge. That's not the same thing.

Professionals run processes. Professionals produce consistent results. Professionals don't have roller coaster months because their performance is anchored in methodology, not in luck.

The Desk Structure: Why It Matters

At the heart of the process sits the desk — the manager who controls the numbers. Understanding the desk is critical for every salesperson.

The desk manager is working with incomplete information unless the salesperson gives them complete information. And the only way to give them complete information is to run the process — specifically, to fill out the write-up sheet before going to the desk.

Think about what the desk needs to make a deal:

- What vehicle is the customer buying?
- What are they trading in, and what's the payoff?
- How much are they putting down?
- What payment are they looking for?
- What's their credit situation?
- Is there an outside approval?

Without this information, the desk manager is guessing. They're building deals on assumptions that may be completely wrong. And when assumptions meet reality — when the customer balks at the payment because it's nothing like what they actually asked for — the deal falls apart and everyone blames each other.

Fill out the sheet before you go to the desk. Every time.

The T.O. (Turn Over) Process

The T.O. — turn over to a manager — is one of the most underutilized tools on the average sales floor.

Many salespeople view the T.O. as an admission of failure. *I couldn't close it, so now the manager has to come clean it up.*

This is exactly backwards.

The T.O. is a process tool. It is a second voice, a fresh perspective, an authority figure who can sometimes do things the salesperson cannot. Used correctly, it is not a rescue operation — it is a deliberate escalation that is part of the designed sequence.

Top salespeople use the T.O. proactively. *"I want to introduce you to my manager before we go through the numbers, just so you know the whole team is working for you."* This reframes the T.O. as a service gesture rather than a pressure tactic.

The result: the manager enters the deal with context, with the sheet filled out, with clear information about what the customer needs — and can often close deals that appeared to be stalled.

Process in a 30-Second Version

If someone asked you to explain why process matters in thirty seconds, here is your answer:

Conversations wander. Processes close deals.

A conversation follows wherever the customer leads. It gets sidetracked. It goes in circles. It ends with "let me think about it" because there was no structure guiding it toward a decision.

A process has a direction. It always knows the next step. It moves forward even when the customer is uncertain, because the process — not the customer's emotional state — defines what happens next.

This is why the worksheet is not paperwork. It is the mechanism that turns a wandering conversation into a process. It is what separates the salesperson who is selling from the one who is just talking.

More on that in the next chapter.

BOTTOM LINE: Process is the foundation of consistent performance. Personality is what makes the process enjoyable. But without the structure — without the Road to the Sale running underneath every interaction

— you are dependent on luck, traffic, and the emotional state of each individual customer. Build the process. Run it every time.

TAKEAWAYS:

- The Road to the Sale is a proven sequence — not a suggestion. Each step exists for a reason.
- Process beats personality for consistent results every time.
- The desk manager can only work with the information you bring. Bring everything.
- The T.O. is a power tool, not a rescue. Use it proactively.
- Conversations wander. Processes close deals.

PART TWO: EVERY DEAL EVERY TIME

CHAPTER 5: EVERY DEAL EVERY TIME — THE PHILOSOPHY

There is a mindset question that separates the salespeople who build careers from the ones who flame out or coast.

The question is this: **Do you believe that consistent process produces better results than selective effort?**

The wrong answer — the one that produces mediocre careers — goes something like this: *I know which customers are serious. I can read people. I only need to run the full process on the ones who are actually going to buy.*

This answer is wrong for reasons that are both psychological and mathematical.

Psychologically, no salesperson is as accurate at reading customers as they believe they are. The signal we think we're reading — "this person looks like a buyer" versus "this person is just looking" — is actually mostly noise. It's pattern matching based on past experience that is riddled with confirmation bias. You have convinced yourself you can predict customer outcomes because you remember the times your prediction was right and forget the times it was wrong.

Mathematically, if you are selectively running your full process — putting in maximum effort on maybe 40% of your customers and coasting through the other 60% — you are cutting your potential commission pool roughly in half. The customers you're coasting on are not all non-buyers. Some of them would buy today if someone ran a proper process on them. But because you decided they weren't worth the effort, you'll never know.

Every Deal Every Time is the commitment to run the full process on every single customer, without exception. No pre-judging. No coasting. No "this one's not serious." Full process, every time.

Why Consistency Beats Talent

Let's be direct about something that the most talented salespeople sometimes resist hearing: in a well-structured sales environment, the most consistent salesperson will outperform the most talented salesperson over any meaningful period of time.

Talent peaks. It produces great days, great weeks, maybe great months. But talent without consistency regresses to the mean. The naturally gifted salesperson who is selective about effort, who only locks in when a deal looks promising, who sometimes just goes through the motions — that person will be beaten in the long run by the disciplined one who runs the same process with the same intensity on every deal every day.

This is not an opinion. It is a documented pattern in every sales environment that tracks performance over time.

The people at the top of the board month after month are not the ones with the most natural ability. They are the ones with the deepest commitment to process. They are the ones who haven't had a "lazy" customer interaction in years because laziness on the floor stopped being an option for them.

Consistency is a competitive advantage. It is not exciting. It is not glamorous. It is the engine that runs the top producers.

The Psychology of Commitment: How Process Turns Shoppers Into Buyers

Here is one of the most powerful concepts in all of behavioral psychology as it applies to sales, and it is exactly what makes the EDET process work.

It is called **commitment and consistency**, and it was articulated most memorably by Dr. Robert Cialdini in his landmark work on influence. The principle is this: once a person takes a small action — makes a small commitment — they are psychologically predisposed to make larger commitments consistent with that first action. The act of committing, even in a minor way, shifts how a person sees themselves in relation to that commitment. They begin to identify as someone who has made this choice.

In sales terms: when a customer takes a small step — gives you their driver's license, writes down their desired payment, tells you their trade payoff — they have crossed a psychological threshold. They have stopped being a browser and started being a participant in the buying process.

Each additional piece of information they provide deepens that commitment. By the time they've given you their down payment amount, their desired monthly payment, their trade information, and their lender's payoff — they have invested mentally and emotionally in the outcome of this interaction. They have skin in the game. Walking away now means accepting that all of that investment produced nothing.

This is not manipulation. The customer always retains the ability to walk away. But human psychology is real, and understanding it makes you a better professional.

The EDET worksheet is an engineered series of small commitments. Every field filled in is a step forward. Every step forward increases the probability of a close. This is why the worksheet is not administrative — it is psychological. It is a closing mechanism disguised as an information form.

The Professional Mindset

Here's what Every Deal Every Time is really asking of you, at its core.

It is asking you to be a professional. Not a nice person. Not a friendly presence on the floor. A professional.

Professionals don't have off days. Professionals don't half-effort because the customer seems like a "be-back." Professionals don't skip the worksheet because it feels awkward to ask for a driver's license.

Professionals run the process. They do it because they understand that the process exists for a reason. They do it because they've seen enough outcomes to know that the ones they can predict with confidence are the ones where they ran every step correctly. They do it because their livelihood and their customers' outcomes depend on them being disciplined enough to do the same thing right, every time.

This is a mindset shift for most salespeople. Selling, from the outside, looks like a personality-driven profession. And many salespeople see themselves primarily as likable people who happen to work at a dealership. The shift to thinking of yourself as a process professional — someone whose value is in their discipline and their methodology, not just their warmth — is the shift that changes careers.

You can be warm and disciplined. You can be personable and process-driven. The best salespeople are both. But if you have to choose which one is running the show, choose process. Every time.

No Exceptions

Here's the hardest part of Every Deal Every Time, and the part that most people intellectually agree with but struggle to actually follow:

No exceptions.

Not for the customer who looks angry when you approach. Not for the customer who says upfront they're definitely not buying today. Not for the customer you personally find difficult. Not for the end of a long Saturday when you're exhausted. Not for the walk-in on a Tuesday afternoon who looks like they're just killing time.

Every customer deserves the full process. Not because you owe it to them out of politeness — because *you owe it to yourself*. Every customer is an opportunity. Every interaction is a chance to close a deal or develop a skill. Treating any of them as less than that is stealing from yourself.

The moment you make an exception — the moment you decide this one isn't worth the full process — you have started a habit. And habits do not stay limited. The exception becomes a pattern. The pattern becomes your default. And your default determines your results.

No exceptions. Every deal. Every time.

BOTTOM LINE: Consistent process is a more reliable source of top performance than talent alone. The EDET mindset demands full effort on every customer, regardless of how "serious" they appear. The psychology of commitment means each step in the process increases the probability of closing. Professionals don't make exceptions.

TAKEAWAYS:

- Selective effort cuts your commission pool nearly in half.
- Consistency beats talent over any meaningful performance period.
- Commitment psychology: small actions lead to larger commitments. Each worksheet field is a step toward the close.
- Being a professional means running the process regardless of how the customer appears.
- No exceptions. The moment you make one, you've started a habit.

CHAPTER 6: THE WORKSHEET IS NOT PAPERWORK

Say it out loud. Actually say it right now, wherever you're reading this.

"The worksheet is not paperwork. The worksheet is a closing tool."

If you can genuinely internalize this reframe — not just say it, but feel it — you will handle this piece of the process completely differently, and your numbers will prove it.

The reason most salespeople are reluctant to use the write-up sheet aggressively is because they think of it as administrative. They think it's something they fill out so the desk manager has the information they need. It's paperwork. You do paperwork after the sale, not before.

This is exactly wrong.

The worksheet is not a data collection form. It is the mechanism by which a shopper becomes a buyer. It is the single most powerful thing you can put in front of a customer who is sitting on the fence. And understanding exactly why each field exists is the key to using it with confidence.

The Shift From Conversation to Process

Remember from Chapter 4: conversations wander. Processes close deals.

Before the worksheet comes out, you are having a conversation. The customer is following their own emotional weather. They're interested, then uncertain, then excited, then worried about their trade, then interested again. The conversation can go anywhere and end anywhere.

The moment the worksheet comes out, you have changed the dynamic of the interaction. You are no longer having a conversation — you are running a process. The worksheet has a structure. It has fields. It moves in a specific direction toward a specific outcome.

The customer feels this shift. Maybe not consciously, but they feel it. The interaction has become more serious. More real. Someone is treating this like a transaction that is actually going to happen.

This is not uncomfortable for serious customers. Serious customers *want* someone to treat their purchase seriously. They walked in here to buy a car. The fact that you're treating the interaction as a real deal rather than just friendly browsing is exactly what they need from you.

The only customers who are uncomfortable when the worksheet comes out are the ones who were never going to buy in the first place. And finding that out quickly is valuable — it frees you to spend your time with the people who are actually going to buy.

Breaking Down Every Field

Let's go through every field on the Every Deal Every Time sheet and explain precisely why it exists — because when you understand the purpose of each element, you can explain it to a customer without hesitation and use it without apology.

Name of Customer

Basic, yes. But it does something important beyond the obvious. Writing down a customer's full name at the top of the sheet formalizes the interaction. It says: *this is a real deal with a real person.* It also starts the commitment process — the customer has now been identified as a participant in this transaction.

Picture of the Driver's License or ID

This is the one that makes most salespeople nervous. "Won't they feel like I'm invading their privacy?"

Here's the reality: the driver's license serves several purposes simultaneously. It provides verified identity for the deal. It provides address verification. It is standard in any legitimate financial transaction, which is exactly what this is. And critically — the act of handing over a government-issued ID is a significant psychological commitment.

Think about the situations in which you hand over your driver's license: renting a car, checking into a hotel, starting a financial transaction. It is not a casual act. It is an act that says *I am serious enough about this to formally identify myself.*

When a customer hands you their ID, they have crossed a significant threshold. The psychological weight of that action tilts them meaningfully toward the close.

Your approach: "I just need to grab a quick photo of your license while we get started — it's how we verify everything and keep things moving quickly on our end." Confident. Matter-of-fact. No hesitation.

Phone Number

This one is straightforward, but its presence on the sheet accomplishes something beyond the obvious follow-up utility. A customer who gives you their phone number has implicitly agreed to communication from you. They've created a thread between this interaction and their life outside the dealership. That thread keeps the deal alive even after they leave.

Money Down

This is the first financial field, and it is where the deal starts to take concrete shape. Asking about down payment early does two things. First, it begins the payment calculation — without knowing the down payment, any conversation about monthly payment is theoretical. Second, it reveals the customer's financial position in a general way, allowing the desk to structure a deal that actually works.

Important: how you ask matters enormously. Not "how much money do you have?" (intrusive) but "Do you have anything you were thinking about putting down to keep the payment lower, or were you thinking about zero down?" This gives them an easy entry point regardless of their answer.

Desired Monthly Payment

This is the most important field on the entire sheet. Here's why.

People do not buy cars based on price. People buy cars based on payment.

This is not an opinion. It is how human beings actually process major purchases. When a person is thinking about whether they can afford a vehicle, they are thinking about their monthly budget — what's coming in, what's going out, and whether they can absorb another payment.

By anchoring the deal to a monthly payment rather than a vehicle price, you have completely changed the nature of the negotiation. Price negotiations are adversarial. The customer wants it lower, you want it higher. Payment discussions are collaborative. You're both trying to figure out how to get the customer into the vehicle they want at a payment they can live with.

When you know the desired payment, the desk can build a deal that targets that number — adjusting term, rate, down payment, and vehicle choice as needed to get there. Without it, you're just throwing numbers at a wall.

Get the desired payment. Always. It is the key that unlocks the entire financial conversation.

Trade Miles and Photos

Documenting the trade early does two critical things. First, it shows the customer you are treating their trade seriously and professionally — you're not just going to eyeball it and throw out a number. Second, it begins the process of establishing the trade's value in a factual way rather than an emotional one.

Customers are almost always emotionally attached to their trade. They have driven it, fixed things on it, associated it with memories. Getting the objective information early — documented mileage, photographic evidence of condition — creates a foundation for the trade conversation that is harder to argue with.

Exact 10-Day Payoff

This field is critical and often skipped, with significant consequences.

Not knowing the trade payoff is one of the most common reasons deals fall apart late. The customer assumed their payoff was one thing; it's actually something else. Or there's a lien they forgot about. Or the payoff has changed since they last looked.

Getting the exact 10-day payoff early means no surprises at the desk. It means the desk manager can see exactly what the real equity situation is and build the deal accordingly. A surprise payoff late in a deal can blow the entire thing up in a way that feels like bad faith, even when nobody was being dishonest.

Ask for it early. "Do you have a rough idea of what you still owe on the trade? Let me grab the exact 10-day payoff number so we have accurate figures — it usually only takes a second."

Exact Name of Trade Lender/Bank

Same principle. Knowing who holds the lien prevents delays and communication breakdowns later in the process. When the desk is trying to put together a deal quickly, having the lender name ready means they can move without waiting for the customer to dig through their paperwork.

Approved Interest Rate and Term of Outside Lender

If the customer has been pre-approved somewhere — a credit union, a personal bank, an online lender — this information is critical. Knowing what rate they came in with tells the desk what they're competing against. If the dealership can match or beat it, great. If not, that information shapes how the deal is structured.

Many salespeople avoid asking this question because they fear it signals that the dealership might lose the financing. The opposite is true: knowing the outside approval lets the desk make a stronger offer, not a weaker one.

Circle Applicable: Real Customer Ready to Purchase / Just Thinking – Need to Look at Other Vehicles

This field is brilliant in its simplicity, and it is perhaps the most underappreciated element of the entire sheet.

By asking the customer to literally identify themselves — are you here to buy today, or are you just thinking? — you accomplish multiple things simultaneously.

You create a moment of honest self-reflection. Many customers who say "I'm just looking" haven't really thought about whether that's true. When they're asked directly to categorize themselves, many will admit — verbally or by their reaction — that they're more serious than they initially presented.

You surface the customers who genuinely are not going to buy today without wasting an hour finding out the hard way.

And you create a shared understanding of the interaction that both parties can move forward from honestly.

If they circle "Real Customer Ready to Purchase" — you are in a deal. Run it.

If they circle "Just Thinking" — you know what you're working with. Your job now is to find out what it would take to move them to "ready," and work toward that.

The Worksheet Makes You Look Like a Professional

Here's a practical reality that most salespeople overlook: when you walk up to a customer with a process — a structured sheet, a clear sequence of questions, a professional methodology — you look completely different from the salesperson who just wandered over and started chatting.

Customers don't get scared when you ask for information. Customers get scared when you don't know what you're doing.

The salesperson who fumbles, who doesn't have a clear next step, who seems unsure whether to go to the desk or stay on the floor — that person makes customers nervous. There's no confidence there. No structure. No sense that this person knows how this process works.

The salesperson who says, clearly and calmly, "The way we do this is we put everything on one sheet so we can see if the numbers make sense for you" — that person looks organized. Authoritative. Like they've done this before. Like they know how to take care of you.

Process projects confidence. Confidence earns trust. Trust closes deals.

Payment vs. Price: The Most Important Reframe in Sales

We said it above but it bears expanding. The EDET sheet anchors the entire conversation around payment, and this is not an accident. It is a deliberate and powerful choice.

When you talk about price, you are talking about a number that is large, fixed, and intimidating. $32,000 is a scary number for most people. It triggers the risk centers of the brain. It invites comparison shopping. It feels like something that needs to be negotiated down.

When you talk about payment, you are talking about a number that is manageable, adjustable, and familiar. $479 per month is a number most people can evaluate against their own budget in real time. They can say "yes, I can do $479" or "I'm really trying to stay at $420" — either way, you're in a productive conversation.

The $32,000 conversation goes: *How low can you go? What's your best price? I saw it for $30,500 online.*

The $479 conversation goes: *What would I need to put down to get there? Is there a longer term? Is there a slightly different vehicle in that payment range?*

One is adversarial. One is collaborative.

The worksheet builds the collaborative conversation by design.

BOTTOM LINE: The EDET worksheet is not an administrative tool. It is the mechanism that transforms a browsing interaction into a buying process. Each field serves a specific purpose — logistical, psychological, or financial — and together they anchor the deal around the only number that really matters to the customer: the monthly payment.

TAKEAWAYS:

- The worksheet changes the interaction from conversation to process.
- Every field exists for a reason — know the reason and you use the field with confidence.

- Asking for a driver's license is a significant psychological commitment that moves the deal forward.
- Desired monthly payment is the most important field — this is how people actually buy.
- Process projects confidence. Confidence earns trust. Trust closes deals.

CHAPTER 7: WHY YOU'RE AFRAID TO USE IT (AND WHY THAT FEAR IS COSTING YOU)

Let's talk about something almost nobody in sales training discusses openly, because it requires admitting something that feels uncomfortable.

Most salespeople know they should use the worksheet more consistently than they do. They've been told. They've seen it work when they did use it. And yet, on any given day, on any given floor, the majority of customer interactions proceed without a completed write-up sheet.

Why?

There are four reasons. Every one of them is costing you money. And every one of them is more about your own psychology than about anything the customer is doing.

Reason 1: Fear of Rejection

"If I ask for their license and payoff too early, I'll scare them away."

This is the most common reason, and it sounds reasonable on the surface. You don't want to come across as aggressive. You don't want to rush a customer who might just need time. You don't want to ask for something they're not ready to give.

But here is what's actually happening under the surface of this thought: you are making a decision based on what protects *you* from the discomfort of rejection, and you are framing it as if it benefits the customer.

It doesn't.

If the customer is going to be scared away by being asked for their driver's license — by being treated like a legitimate buyer in a legitimate financial transaction — they were almost certainly not going to buy today regardless. That information is useful. You want to know it early, not forty-five minutes into an interaction.

If the customer isn't scared off — and most won't be, because being treated professionally is not scary — you've moved the deal forward significantly.

The fear of asking for the driver's license is not concern for the customer's experience. It is concern for your own ego. The salesperson who doesn't ask avoids the small risk of a customer's momentary irritation. But they accept the much larger risk of losing the deal entirely.

Safe salespeople don't close deals. The comfort zone in this business is a poverty zone. Every time you choose not to push the process forward because you're afraid of how the customer might react, you are trading a commission for a moment of safety.

That's an extraordinarily bad trade.

Reason 2: Fear of Being Pushy

Many salespeople — particularly those who are genuinely empathetic, relationship-oriented people — carry a specific anxiety about sales. They don't want to be *that guy*. The high-pressure, won't-take-no-for-an-answer, relentless closer who makes customers feel trapped.

This anxiety is healthy in appropriate doses. Genuinely manipulative, high-pressure tactics that override customers' best interests are not good sales. They produce unhappy customers, bad reviews, chargebacks, and reputational damage.

But here is where many salespeople go wrong: they apply that anxiety not just to manipulative tactics, but to the entire professional structure of the sales process. They conflate being organized and process-driven with being pushy. They feel that any kind of forward momentum — any redirection of the customer toward the next step — is somehow aggressive.

It is not.

Customers don't buy from followers. Customers buy from professionals who guide them.

Think about the last time you went to a doctor, a lawyer, an accountant, a financial advisor. Did the professional say "let me know if you have any questions" and then back away while you wandered around their office? Of course not. They guided you through a process. They asked you questions. They directed you toward the next step. And you didn't feel manipulated — you felt served.

A salesperson who guides a customer through the buying process — who says "here's what we need to do next, here's why it helps you, and here's how we move forward" — is not being pushy. They are being a professional.

The confusion between professional guidance and high-pressure manipulation is one of the most expensive mistakes in sales.

Reframe "pushy" as "structured." Reframe "aggressive" as "organized." Reframe "pressure" as "direction."

You are not pushing customers. You are doing your job.

Reason 3: They Don't Understand What the Worksheet Is For

A significant number of salespeople — particularly newer ones — genuinely think the write-up sheet is administrative. They think it's something the desk manager needs to build the deal. They think it comes later in the process, after the customer has already decided they want to buy.

This misunderstanding leads to a devastating sequence: the salesperson spends an hour with the customer, builds rapport, does the demo drive, the customer expresses interest — and *then* the salesperson goes to get the write-up sheet. At which point the customer's emotional state has peaked and begun its descent. At which point the next step feels like paperwork, not progress. At which point the customer says "let me just take this home and think about it."

The write-up sheet is not administrative. **The write-up sheet is a closing tool.**

It belongs in the first ten to fifteen minutes of the serious conversation — after the needs assessment, after the vehicle has been identified, but long before the emotional peak has been reached. It belongs right at the moment when the customer has enough emotional investment to participate, but the deal hasn't reached the critical moment yet.

When salespeople understand that filling out the worksheet *is* the close — that the act of filling it out moves the customer from shopper to buyer — they stop treating it like an afterthought and start treating it like the weapon it actually is.

Burn this into memory: **The worksheet is how you turn a shopper into a buyer. Not paperwork. A closing tool.**

Reason 4: Laziness and Lack of Confidence

This one is the most honest and the hardest to hear.

Some salespeople don't use the worksheet because they don't know what to say. They haven't rehearsed the introduction. They stumble when they try to ask for the license. They don't have smooth answers when the customer pushes back. So they default to the path of least resistance: they don't ask.

This is laziness masquerading as sensitivity. And it is the fastest route to a career of mediocre numbers.

The salesperson who doesn't know what to say needs to learn what to say. That's it. The word tracks are not complicated. The explanations are not difficult. The responses to objections are learnable. Chapter 8 is going to give you exactly what to say and exactly how to say it.

But first: you have to be willing to do the work of learning them. You have to be willing to practice until they feel natural. You have to be willing to deploy them even when you feel uncertain, because the only way uncertainty becomes confidence is by acting through it repeatedly.

"**Default: let me know if you have any questions.**"

This sentence — this resignation from the sales process — is the calling card of the salesperson who has given up. Every time you say it, you are broadcasting to the customer: *I don't have a next step, I don't know how to advance this, and I've decided it's your job to figure out what happens next.*

Customers who hear that sentence almost never generate a productive question. They wander the floor and they leave.

You have a next step. You always have a next step. It is spelled out in the Road to the Sale. It is defined by where you are in the process. You never have to say "let me know if you have any questions" because you always know what the next step is.

The Cost of the Four Fears

Let's make this concrete. If you have 20 customer interactions in a month, and you only use the full EDET process on 8 of them because the other 12 felt too uncertain, too early, too uncomfortable — you have reduced your potential deal pool by 60%.

At an average gross of $2,000 per deal and a reasonable closing rate of 25% on a full process, the difference between running the process on 8 deals versus 20 is potentially three or four additional commissions per month. Every month. Twelve months a year.

Over the course of a career, the four fears cost some salespeople hundreds of thousands of dollars.

That is not an exaggeration. It is math.

The question is never whether you should run the process. The question is whether you're willing to feel slightly uncomfortable for the time it takes to make it automatic.

BOTTOM LINE: The four fears — rejection, being pushy, misunderstanding the tool's purpose, and lack of confidence — are internal obstacles, not customer signals. Each one is a choice to protect your comfort at the expense of your results. The professional reframes pushy as structured, rejection as information, and the worksheet as a weapon.

TAKEAWAYS:

- Fear of rejection is protecting your ego at the expense of your commission.

- Customers buy from professionals who guide them, not followers who accommodate them.
- The worksheet is a closing tool, not paperwork — it belongs early in the process.
- "Let me know if you have any questions" is the white flag of the professional sales interaction.
- The math of process avoidance is brutal: four fears, practiced consistently, can cost hundreds of thousands of dollars over a career.

CHAPTER 8: THE WORD TRACK THAT CLOSES THE GAP

You know what to do. You know why to do it. You know what happens when you don't.

Now let's talk about exactly what to say.

This is a chapter of precision. Scripts. Word tracks. Actual language you can use beginning today. Not suggestions. Templates. Take them, make them yours, practice them until they sound natural coming out of your mouth.

The biggest mistake salespeople make with word tracks is reading them robotically. A script is a structure — it gives you the shape of what to say and the key points to hit. Your own voice, your own energy, your own timing fills in the rest. Practice until the words are automatic and your attention is free to focus on the customer's reaction.

The Master Word Track

This is the all-purpose, every-situation introduction to the EDET sheet. Memorize it. Then adapt it to your voice.

"I don't want to waste your time or mine going back and forth. If you like the vehicle, the next step is we just put everything on one sheet and see if the numbers make sense for you. Takes about three minutes and it'll tell us whether we're in the right range."

Note what this does:

- Positions the worksheet as efficiency, not bureaucracy.
- Uses "we" — collaborative, not adversarial.
- Frames it as informational ("see if the numbers make sense") rather than conclusive.
- Gives a time investment (three minutes) that is non-threatening.

Variation: "**The way we make this easy is we put everything on one sheet so we can see if the numbers work for you. If they do, great. If they don't, no problem. But this will save you a lot of time.**"

This variation adds the "no problem if it doesn't work" frame — which paradoxically reduces resistance because the customer doesn't feel trapped.

Scenario 1: The First-Time Buyer

First-time buyers are simultaneously the easiest and most nerve-wracking customers. Easy because they don't have preconceived notions of how the process should go. Nerve-wracking because they're anxious and unfamiliar.

Your approach should be warm, clear, and structured. They want to be guided — they just don't want to be taken advantage of.

Salesperson: "Have you ever purchased a vehicle before, or is this your first time?"

Customer: "First time, yeah. I'm a little nervous about the whole thing honestly."

Salesperson: "Completely normal. What we're going to do is make this as straightforward as possible — I'm going to walk you through every step. First, let me show you a couple of options based on what you told me. Then once you find one you like, we're going to sit down and put everything on one sheet together — your payment goal, what you're putting down, all of it — so you can see exactly what you're looking at before any decisions are made. Nothing happens without you knowing the full picture first. Sound good?"

Customer: "Yeah, that works."

You've just introduced the worksheet without the worksheet even being visible yet. The customer has agreed to the process before you've started it. When the time comes to fill it out, it won't feel like a surprise.

Scenario 2: The Skeptical Customer

The skeptical customer has been to dealers before. They've been through the games, the "let me check with my manager" shuffle, the four-square nightmare. They come in guarded, with their defenses up.

Your job is not to fight the defenses. Your job is to make them irrelevant by being completely transparent about your process.

Salesperson: "I can tell you've been through this before."

Customer: "More than I wanted to. Just tell me your best price and we'll go from there."

Salesperson: "Here's what I'll do — instead of playing the pricing game, let me show you something different. We're going to put everything on one sheet right now — your trade, your payment target, your down payment — and I'll show you exactly where we land and exactly what's included. No back and forth. No mystery numbers. You'll see the full picture up front, and if it works, great. If it doesn't, I'll tell you straight up. Fair?"

The skeptical customer respects directness. By offering full transparency and framing the worksheet as the antidote to the games they've experienced before, you've made process your selling point.

Scenario 3: The Trade-In Customer

The trade-in customer often walks in with one thing on their mind: what am I going to get for my trade? Everything else is secondary until that question is answered.

Here's the key: don't compete with the trade question. Use it as the entry point to the worksheet.

Customer: "Before we do anything, I want to know what you're going to give me for my car."

Salesperson: "Absolutely, we're going to get that figured out for you — that's actually one of the most important pieces. What I need from you is a quick look at it and a few numbers on your end. Pull up your lender's app or give them a call — I just need your exact 10-day payoff. While you do that, let me get some photos and the mileage, and we'll have everything ready so when we sit down with the numbers, your trade is already factored in."

Notice: you haven't avoided the trade question. You've engaged it directly and made it a reason to start the worksheet process. The customer feels heard. The process is now running.

Scenario 4: The "Just Looking" Customer

The "just looking" customer is the most common customer type and the one that most salespeople mishandle. The response to "just looking" should never be "okay, let me know if you have any questions."

Customer: "We're just looking right now. We're not really ready to buy."

Salesperson: "No problem at all. What kind of vehicle are you looking for? I'll show you what we have in your range."

[Thirty minutes later, after vehicle selection and demo drive]

Salesperson: "All right, I know you said you were just looking, but you looked like you enjoyed that one. Let me ask — is it more the timing, the payment, or something specific about the vehicle that's holding you back?"

Customer: "Honestly, I just don't know what my payment would be."

Salesperson: "That's exactly what I want to figure out for you. You don't have to decide anything today — let me just put everything together on one sheet so at least you know what the real number looks like. Takes three minutes. Would that be helpful?"

Almost every "just looking" customer has a specific thing preventing them from moving forward today. Find it. Then use the worksheet to address it.

Scenario 5: The Payment-Sensitive Customer

The payment-sensitive customer has a hard number in their head — often one they've gotten from an online calculator or a vague sense of what they can afford. They lead with it almost immediately.

Customer: "I need to stay under $400 a month."

Salesperson: "Let's make sure we hit that for you — I want to know what you're working with so I can make sure we're looking at the right vehicles. Here's what I'm going to do: let me grab a few quick things from you — your down payment, the payoff on your current vehicle if you have one, and whether you have any financing in place already. Once I have that, I can tell you pretty quickly whether we can get to $400 or close to it, and if we can't, I'll tell you straight. Sound good?"

The payment-sensitive customer is actually your easiest customer if you anchor the entire conversation in their payment. That is what the worksheet is designed to do. Use it aggressively.

Handling the Most Common Objections

"I'm not comfortable giving you my driver's license."

"Completely understand. I just need it to verify your information and keep things moving — it's the same thing any financial transaction requires. I'll take a quick photo and hand it right back. You can watch me the whole time."

If they still won't provide it: note it and move on. You'll address it with the "Just Thinking" circle at the end. But in most cases, confident matter-of-fact delivery prevents this objection entirely.

"Why do you need my payoff?"

"Because without the exact payoff, any number I give you on the trade value is going to be incomplete. If there's more equity than I think, that's money in your pocket. If it's less, I'd rather we know now than at the end. I want to give you accurate information."

"I don't know my payment target — I'll know it when I see a number."

"I get it. Let me ask it differently: what are you paying on your current vehicle?" [They answer.] "Okay, and would you like to go higher, lower, or about the same?" [They answer.] "Perfect, that's our target."

You've gotten a payment target through the side door. Add it to the sheet.

The One Phrase You Must Kill

"Let me know if you have any questions."

Write this phrase on a piece of paper, cross it out, and throw it away. It does not exist in your vocabulary anymore.

Every time you are about to say "let me know if you have any questions," stop yourself and replace it with one of these:

- "What do you think — did it feel like the right fit?"
- "Let me show you the inside while we're here."
- "I know you said payment is the key thing — let's sit down and figure out exactly what that looks like."
- "Let me introduce you to my manager real quick so you can meet the whole team."

You always have a next step. Use it.

BOTTOM LINE: Word tracks are not scripts to recite — they are structures to internalize. Know the purpose behind each phrase, make it your own, and deploy it confidently. The salesperson with practiced word tracks moves deals forward in every scenario. The salesperson who wings it gets different results every time.

TAKEAWAYS:

- The master word track positions the worksheet as efficiency, not pressure.
- Every customer type has a tailored approach — first-time, skeptical, trade-in, just looking, payment-sensitive.
- Common objections to providing information have simple, honest, confident responses.
- "Let me know if you have any questions" must be eliminated entirely from your vocabulary.
- Practice word tracks until they're automatic — your attention should be on the customer, not the words.

CHAPTER 9: REAL CUSTOMERS VS. TIRE KICKERS — HOW TO KNOW IMMEDIATELY

Here is one of the things that nobody talks about openly enough in sales training: not everyone who walks onto your lot is going to buy a car. Some people are genuinely there to browse. Some people are trying to figure out what they want before they're ready to commit. Some people walked in because it was raining outside and they needed a place to be.

This is not a problem. It's reality. And the EDET process is designed to surface this reality quickly — before you spend forty-five minutes on a demo drive and a full walkaround with someone who was never going to buy today.

The ability to identify who is actually ready to purchase — and to do it within the first fifteen minutes of an interaction — is one of the most valuable skills you can develop. Not because you should dismiss anyone who isn't ready today. But because understanding where each customer actually is allows you to deploy your energy correctly and have honest, productive conversations.

The Real Customer Signals

A customer who is genuinely ready to purchase today will exhibit a consistent set of behaviors. They may not announce it — many will still say "just looking" as a reflex even when they're absolutely there to buy. But their actions tell a different story.

They ask specific questions. Not "what models do you have?" but "does this one come in blue?" Not "how does financing work?" but "what would my payment be if I put two thousand down?" Specific questions mean a specific purchase intention.

They bring information. They know their trade payoff. They have a recent credit check. They've looked at their budget. They've compared the vehicle to competitors online. People who are "just looking" don't do homework.

They engage physically. They open doors, look at the trunk, sit in the driver's seat, adjust the mirrors, check the USB ports. Physical engagement is emotional investment. The tire kicker keeps their distance.

Their timeline has urgency. "My lease is up in six weeks." "Our third kid was just born and we need the room now." "My transmission died yesterday." Urgency creates buyers. When there's no urgency, there's no timeline, and without a timeline, decisions don't get made.

They want to take the demo drive. Casual browsers often don't. They look at the outside, ask a few questions, and move on. Real buyers want to feel the vehicle, because they're already imagining ownership.

They respond constructively to the worksheet. When you introduce the EDET sheet, a real buyer engages.

They pull out their phone to check their payoff. They think about their down payment. They tell you what payment they're looking for. They are willing to participate in the process because the process is moving toward what they want.

The Tire Kicker Signals

The tire kicker is not a bad person. They may be a future customer. They may simply not be ready today. But you need to identify them quickly so you can have an honest conversation about what they actually need.

They ask vague, general questions. "What kind of gas mileage does this get?" is fine. "What are all the different models you carry?" followed by no follow-up questions — just browsing — is a different signal.

They resist providing information. When you introduce the EDET sheet, the tire kicker stiffens. They don't want to give their phone number. They'll tell you they don't know their payoff. They're reluctant to name a payment target because "it depends on the price" —

and not in the honest way of someone who's done the math.

They talk about future timing. "We're thinking about doing this in the fall." "Once I get my tax return." "We're not in a rush." These are not deal-killers on their own — someone with a genuine three-month timeline is worth staying in contact with. But combined with other signals, they indicate today is not the day.

They're gathering information for a decision, not making one. There's a category of customer who has done a lot of research, is narrowing down their options, and is visiting multiple dealerships today to compare. This customer is not a tire kicker exactly — they may well buy within the week. But they are not buying today. Identify this quickly and manage the interaction accordingly.

They don't engage physically. They look from a distance. They ask about the car without touching it. They seem more interested in the conversation than the vehicle.

The EDET Sheet as the Sorting Mechanism

Here is the beautiful efficiency of the worksheet: it does the sorting for you.

When you introduce the EDET sheet — calmly, professionally, early in the interaction — the customer's response tells you everything. There is no more reliable signal than how a customer reacts to being asked to participate in the buying process.

Real buyers lean in. They might have a question or two, they might need to look something up, but fundamentally they say yes — because the process is moving toward what they want.

Tire kickers lean back. They hesitate. They create distance. They say "I don't really know yet" to questions that anyone seriously considering buying today would have answers to.

This is not a test you're giving them. You are not trying to catch them out. You are genuinely trying to figure out how to help them. The worksheet is the most honest possible way to have that conversation: *here's what we need to figure out if we're going to make this work. Are you there?*

What to Do When They Won't Provide Information

When a customer resists the worksheet — won't give the license, won't give the payoff, won't name a payment target — you have a choice. You can back off completely (which signals to the customer that it was optional all along, and the process dies). Or you can address it directly.

The direct approach:

"I completely understand if you're not there yet. Can I ask — is it the vehicle, the timing, or the numbers that are making you hesitant?"

You're not pressuring. You're diagnosing. Most hesitation comes from one of three sources: they don't love the vehicle enough yet, the timing isn't quite right, or they're worried the numbers won't work. Each of these is addressable.

If the vehicle isn't right: go back to the needs assessment and find a better match. Run the process on a different vehicle.

If the timing isn't right: get a solid follow-up scheduled, find out the specific date things change for them, and become their resource for that moment.

If they're worried the numbers won't work: "The only way to know if the numbers work is to put them together. You might be surprised. Let's just see." This is almost always worth trying. Customers routinely assume they can't afford something and are pleasantly surprised when the deal is structured correctly.

Respecting Your Own Time

Here is a principle that newer salespeople often resist but that seasoned professionals understand deeply: your time has value.

When you spend sixty minutes with a customer who is never going to buy today, you have used sixty minutes that could have gone to a customer who would. This is not about dismissing anyone. It is about being honest with yourself about where you're creating value.

The EDET process allows you to identify the real buyers within fifteen to twenty minutes. For the ones who aren't ready today, you can have a shorter, high-value conversation — gather their information, schedule a follow-up, make sure they know you're their resource — and move on. You don't need to abandon them. You need to right-size the interaction.

The manager who says "**If we don't have this sheet filled out, we don't have a deal**" is not being harsh. They are protecting everyone's time, including the customer's.

Real buyers want a deal to happen. Real buyers will participate in the process. Real buyers don't make filling out a simple information sheet feel like pulling teeth.

The "Just Thinking" Circle: Using Honesty as a Tool

That final field on the EDET sheet — the one that asks the customer to self-identify as either "Real Customer Ready to Purchase" or "Just thinking – need to look at other vehicles" — is one of the most powerful closing questions disguised as paperwork.

When you reach this field, pause. Don't skip over it. Let the customer actually engage with it.

"And the last thing — this is just to help me serve you the right way. Would you say you're in a position where if the numbers make sense today, you'd be ready to move forward? Or are you earlier in the process and need to look around more first?"

A customer who says "if the numbers work, I'd do it today" just gave you everything you need. They've committed to buying today on one condition: the numbers. Your entire job from this moment is to make the numbers work.

A customer who says "I really need to look around more" is giving you honest information. Thank them for it. Find out what they're comparing. Establish yourself as the resource. Get a follow-up scheduled.

Either way, you know exactly where you are. And knowing exactly where you are is far better than guessing.

BOTTOM LINE: Not every customer is a buyer today, and the EDET process is the fastest and most honest way to find out which ones are. The worksheet is your sorting mechanism — it separates real buyers from browsers within fifteen minutes. When customers won't engage with the process, diagnose the hesitation directly instead of backing off.

TAKEAWAYS:

- Real customers ask specific questions, bring information, engage physically, and respond constructively to the worksheet.
- Tire kickers ask vague questions, resist providing information, and talk about future timing.
- The worksheet's response is the most reliable commitment signal you have.
- When someone won't engage, diagnose: is it the vehicle, the timing, or the numbers?

- Your time has value. Right-size interactions based on where the customer actually is.

CHAPTER 10: THE DESK MANAGER'S PERSPECTIVE

Everything we've discussed so far has been about what happens on the floor — the interaction between salesperson and customer. But there's another critical player in every deal: the desk manager.

If you want to understand why the EDET process matters so completely, spend a week at the desk. Watch what happens when a salesperson walks up with a fully completed sheet versus when one walks up with a vehicle number and a shrug.

The difference is not subtle.

What Happens at the Desk

The desk manager's job is to take the information a salesperson brings and build a deal structure —

pricing, trade value, financing, payments — that satisfies both the dealership's margin requirements and the customer's needs. It is a complex, real-time puzzle that depends entirely on the quality of information fed into it.

When a salesperson walks to the desk with:

- Customer name
- Verified driver's license / ID
- Phone number
- Down payment amount
- Desired monthly payment
- Trade vehicle with accurate mileage and photos
- Exact 10-day payoff
- Trade lender name
- Any outside financing approval

...the desk manager can build an accurate, customer-specific deal structure in three to five minutes. They can see immediately what the real equity picture looks like, whether the payment target is achievable, what adjustments might be needed, and what the strongest possible offer is. They can send the salesperson back with a real number — a number that has a real chance of closing.

When a salesperson walks to the desk with:

- "The customer wants to trade their car."
- "I think they owe somewhere around twelve grand, but I'm not sure."
- "They said they want to keep payments low."
- [No down payment discussed]
- [No payment target established]
- [No outside approval mentioned]

...the desk manager is guessing. They will build a deal based on assumptions that may not match reality at all. The number they send back may hit in the right range and close, or it may be so far off that the customer feels the whole interaction was a waste of their time.

More often than not, it's the second outcome.

The Manager's Honest Assessment

Here's what experienced desk managers say about this privately, because they rarely say it directly in meetings: **weak salespeople waste everyone's time, including the customer's.**

It's not about being cruel. It's about reality. When a salesperson has not run the process — has not filled out the sheet, has not gathered the basic information — the desk cannot do its job effectively. The deal becomes a guessing game. Multiple trips back and forth between the floor and the desk. Numbers that change. Customers who feel jerked around. Gross that erodes because nobody knows where the real flexibility is.

Compare that to a salesperson who walks up to the desk with a fully loaded sheet. That interaction takes five minutes. The desk manager says: "Okay, trade payoff is $14,200, they're putting down $2,000, they want $450 a month, and they've already been approved at 6.9% at their credit union. Tell me — can we beat that rate and hit the payment?" That's a solvable puzzle. That manager can work with that.

Strong salespeople work deals. Weak salespeople present cars.

There is a world of difference between the two. The salesperson who presents a car goes through the motions — shows the vehicle, does the demo, talks about features — and then brings the customer to the desk with essentially nothing done. The salesperson who works a deal has done the work before they ever go to the desk. The desk just needs to execute on the information already gathered.

The desk manager wants the second type of salesperson on their floor. And so does every other manager, because that salesperson makes everyone's job easier and more profitable.

The Manager's Rule

"If we don't have this sheet filled out, we don't have a deal."

This is not a suggestion. In well-run dealerships, it is policy. A salesperson who approaches the desk without a completed EDET sheet gets sent back to the floor to fill it out before numbers are discussed.

This policy exists not to punish salespeople but to protect the integrity of the deal and the customer's experience. An incomplete sheet means incomplete information. Incomplete information means a deal built on guesswork. A deal built on guesswork collapses somewhere — at the desk, in F&I, or at delivery. Better to build the foundation correctly upfront than to patch a crumbling deal at the worst possible moment.

If your dealership doesn't have this policy, you should run the process anyway — because you are the one who suffers from not having the information. Your commissions depend on deals that close. Deals that close are built on complete information.

What Managers Wish Salespeople Understood

A decade of desk experience distills into a few key wishes:

1. The trade payoff matters more than you think.

More deals fall apart at the trade payoff than at any other single point. Customer estimates their payoff at

$10,000. Actual payoff is $13,500. That $3,500 gap just blew up the deal's equity position and the customer feels surprised and misled. Get the exact 10-day payoff. Always. Non-negotiable.

2. Payment, not price.

When a salesperson presents a customer with "they want to pay as little as possible," the desk has nothing to work with. When they present with "they want to be at $450 a month and they're putting down $3,000," the desk has a target. Always anchor to a specific payment.

3. Pre-approval changes everything.

If a customer has been pre-approved at a credit union at a competitive rate, the desk needs to know this before building the deal — not after the customer mentions it when signing paperwork. Knowing about the outside approval changes how financing is presented and whether the dealer can compete on rate. Surface it early.

4. Don't negotiate on the way to the desk.

Some salespeople — trying to be helpful, or trying to avoid conflict — will make commitments about price or trade value before the deal has been structured. "I'm sure we can get you close to that." "I'll see what we can do on the trade." These informal commitments create a baseline in the customer's mind that makes the real numbers harder to land.

Do not negotiate before the desk has the numbers. Your job is to gather information and present the deal. The desk's job is to structure it.

How to Be the Salesperson Managers Fight to Keep

Every desk manager has a short list of salespeople they go to bat for. The ones who get better traffic, more support, more flexibility when deals are complicated. Here is exactly how to get on that list:

Come to the desk with everything. Every time. No excuses.

Be honest about the deal. If the customer was difficult, say so. If there's a challenge with the trade, name it.

Managers can solve problems they know about. Surprises kill deals.

Run the process all the way through before the desk is involved. The desk should never have to ask "did you get the payoff?" or "what are they looking to put down?" Those answers should be on the sheet in front of them.

Follow up quickly after desk touchbacks. When the manager sends you back with a counter, move. Don't leave the customer waiting while you take a detour through the break room.

Be easy to send deals to. The desk will send you more of them.

BOTTOM LINE: The desk manager can only build deals from the information provided. A complete EDET sheet is the difference between a deal that closes in one round and a deal that dies in three. Strong salespeople work deals before they ever reach the desk. That's what makes them valuable.

TAKEAWAYS:

- A complete EDET sheet lets the desk build an accurate deal in five minutes. An incomplete one produces guesswork.
- Trade payoff surprises cause more deal collapses than any other single factor.
- Always anchor to a specific payment target, not a vague desire to "keep payments low."
- Never negotiate price or trade value before the desk has the complete picture.
- Be easy to work with at the desk — it determines how much support you get.

CHAPTER 11: CONTROLLING THE CONVERSATION WITHOUT CONTROLLING THE CUSTOMER

There is a tension at the heart of every sales interaction that most salespeople never fully resolve. On one hand, you need to guide the conversation — to keep it moving forward, to maintain structure, to prevent the customer from wandering off into doubt or distraction. On the other hand, you are working with a human being who has their own priorities, their own concerns, and their own pace.

The resolution of this tension is what separates truly great salespeople from the rest.

It is not about controlling the customer. It is about controlling the process.

The Difference Between Control and Manipulation

Manipulation is when you use techniques to override a customer's better judgment — to push them past a genuine concern, to use pressure tactics that create false urgency, to obscure information that would lead to a different decision.

Control — in the professional sense — is when you understand the customer's goal better than they do in this moment and guide the interaction toward achieving it.

Here's an example. A customer walks in wanting a specific model. Thirty minutes into the interaction, it's clear that model doesn't fit their needs — wrong size for their family, wrong payment range for their budget. A manipulative salesperson pushes the model anyway, because they want to close the deal they have in front of them. A controlling professional says: "Based on what you told me — three kids, two car seats, a 45-minute commute — I actually think this one might serve you better. Let me show you why."

That is control in service of the customer. That is the right kind of control.

Professional process feels like service, not pressure. When the process is running correctly, the customer doesn't feel managed — they feel taken care of. They feel like they're working with someone who knows what they're doing and has their best interest at heart. That's the goal.

Questions as Steering Tools

The most powerful tool for keeping a conversation moving in the right direction is something you already have and use constantly: questions.

Questions do something remarkable in a sales conversation. They redirect attention, they advance the process, and they help the customer feel like they are in control — even when you are actually guiding every step. There is no adversarial moment in a well-crafted question.

Here are some examples of questions used as steering tools:

Moving from browsing to needs assessment:

"What's the main thing you're trying to fix with your current vehicle?"

This question takes the customer from passive browsing to active problem-solving. Now they're thinking about what they need, and you have information to work with.

Moving from needs assessment to vehicle selection:

"Based on what you told me, this one is going to be the best fit — but let me show you one more option so you have a comparison. Can I grab the keys?"

This question moves the interaction without pressure. You're adding value (the comparison) while advancing the process (heading toward the vehicle selection step).

Moving from vehicle selection to the worksheet:

"You said the payment is the key thing for you — do you want to at least see what the numbers look like? It'll take us three minutes."

This question uses the customer's own stated priority (payment) as the reason to start the worksheet. The customer feels like *their* goal is driving the next step, not yours.

Moving from worksheet to the desk:

"I have everything I need to put this together for you. Let me go check with my manager and get you some actual numbers — I'll be right back."

Clean. Direct. Moves the deal forward without ambiguity.

Keeping the Deal Alive When Momentum Drops

Every deal has moments where the momentum drops. The customer goes quiet. They seem distracted. They say something like "I don't know, this is a big decision."

These are not stop signs. They are inflection points — moments where the right intervention keeps the deal alive and the wrong one lets it die.

The wrong intervention: silence, backing off, "take all the time you need."

The right intervention: **a direct, empathetic question that surfaces the real hesitation.**

"I hear you — it is a big decision. Can I ask: is it the payment that's making you hesitant, or is it something about the vehicle itself?"

This question does three things: it validates the customer's feeling (which reduces defensiveness), it narrows the hesitation to a specific cause (which makes it addressable), and it keeps the conversation going (which keeps the deal alive).

There is almost always something specific behind "this is a big decision." A concern about the trade. A worry about rate. An unconvinced spouse. A budget anxiety they haven't fully named yet. Find the specific. Address the specific. The deal gets back on track.

The Art of the Purposeful Pause

Control doesn't mean constant forward pressure. Sometimes the most powerful thing you can do is pause — deliberately and strategically — after a key question or statement. Give the customer room to respond. Don't rush to fill the silence.

The salesperson who can sit with a moment of silence after saying "if the numbers work for you today, is there anything stopping you from moving forward?" is more powerful than the one who talks the moment the sentence is finished. The silence creates space for the customer to say yes. Talking through it fills that space with noise.

Learn to use silence as a tool. Ask the question. Stop. Wait. Let the customer respond.

The Handoff Between Salesperson and Desk

One of the most underestimated skills in automotive sales is the quality of the handoff between the salesperson and the desk manager. Done well, the handoff reinforces the deal, adds authority to the process, and signals to the customer that the team is organized and working for them. Done poorly, it creates confusion, undermines the salesperson's credibility, and gives the customer a chance to retrench.

The best handoffs are structured and enthusiastic.

Salesperson: "I've got everything we need to put this together. Before I go check on the numbers, I want to introduce you to my manager — just so you know the whole team is in your corner here."

The manager enters, shakes hands, reinforces the salesperson's work: "I hear you found the right one. Let me take a look at everything and see what we can do for you."

Two things have happened: the manager has been introduced before numbers come up (making the introduction a relationship move, not a pressure escalation), and the customer feels like the whole dealership is invested in making their deal work.

The T.O. — the formal turn-over to the manager — is a powerful closing tool when done with warmth and professionalism. Use it intentionally.

What Professional Control Looks Like to the Customer

Here's the test: after a well-run sales interaction, the customer should not feel pushed. They should feel helped.

They should feel like they worked with someone who understood their needs, respected their time, was honest with them about the numbers, and guided them efficiently through a process that ended in a decision they feel good about.

That is what professional process control produces. Not a customer who was talked into something. A customer who was helped to something they wanted and needed.

That distinction is everything. The customers who feel helped come back. They refer their friends. They leave five-star reviews. They buy their next vehicle from you.

The customers who feel pushed? They don't come back. They write the negative review. They tell everyone they know. They are the ones the industry has been fighting to overcome for decades.

Run the process. Guide, don't push. Serve, don't manipulate. The results will follow.

BOTTOM LINE: Professional control means managing the process, not the person. Questions steer the conversation without pressure. Purposeful pauses give customers room to commit. The handoff to the desk, done well, is a relationship tool that adds momentum. The goal is a customer who feels helped, not pushed.

TAKEAWAYS:

- Control the process, not the person. These are completely different things.
- Questions are your steering tools — they advance the deal while keeping the customer feeling in control.
- "This is a big decision" is always covering a specific concern. Find it.
- Purposeful silence after a close question is more powerful than filling it.
- A well-executed T.O. adds authority and warmth. Use it proactively, not as a last resort.

CHAPTER 12: ADAPTING THESE PRINCIPLES BEYOND THE DEALERSHIP

Let's step off the lot for a moment.

Everything in this book — the philosophy of Time Kills Deals, the discipline of Every Deal Every Time, the psychology of commitment, the power of process control — is not specific to automotive sales. These principles apply with equal force to every high-ticket sales environment where a human being is guiding another human being toward a significant financial decision.

Real estate. Insurance. Financial planning. Home improvement contracting. B2B enterprise sales. Medical equipment. Solar energy. Anything where the stakes are high, the decision is complex, and a professional guide makes the difference between a closed deal and a lost one.

The packaging changes. The psychology doesn't.

Why High-Ticket Sales All Work the Same Way

Here is the fundamental truth about any sale involving a significant sum of money: the customer is experiencing some version of the same emotional journey.

There is desire (I want the thing). There is anxiety (this is a lot of money). There is uncertainty (how do I know this is the right choice?). There is social pressure (what will my family think? Am I being smart?). And there is inertia (it's easier not to decide today).

The sales professional's job — regardless of industry — is to move the customer through this journey efficiently and honestly. Urgency reduces inertia. Process reduces anxiety. Good questions surface uncertainty. Commitment psychology builds momentum toward the decision.

These mechanisms work on human beings. And human beings buy real estate and insurance and financial plans and solar panels with the same cognitive and emotional hardware they use to buy cars.

Real Estate: Every Listing, Every Showing

The Time Kills Deals principle is arguably more critical in real estate than in any other industry. Houses move. The customer who wants to "think about it" for a week will often think about it right out of a listing that sold on Thursday.

Urgency in real estate is honest urgency — the market is real, the inventory is real, the competition from other buyers is real. The agent who communicates this clearly and professionally is doing their client a service. The agent who says "take all the time you need" and lets a serious buyer walk away from the right property is failing them.

The EDET equivalent in real estate is the buyer's profile and the pre-qualification document. Before showing anyone a property, the professional agent has:

- Pre-qualification or pre-approval in hand
- Clear understanding of the buyer's maximum comfortable payment
- Down payment amount
- Timeline for purchase
- Non-negotiable criteria vs. nice-to-haves
- Prior purchase or lease history

An agent who shows properties to anyone who expresses interest, without gathering this information first, is running open house showings, not a sales process. They're generating experiences, not transactions.

The word track translates directly: "**Before we look at anything, let me ask you a few quick questions so we don't waste your time showing you properties that don't fit. This takes about ten minutes and it'll make every showing way more useful for you.**"

That's Every Deal Every Time in real estate language.

Insurance: Every Consultation Counts

Insurance sales is perhaps the industry most plagued by the Time Kills Deals problem — because the urgency is invisible. Nobody is dying today (hopefully). Nobody's house is on fire right now. The risk that insurance protects against doesn't feel immediate until it's real.

The insurance professional's challenge is to create appropriate urgency around a protection decision that feels optional in the present moment.

The technique: make the cost of not deciding concrete.

"I understand you want to think about it. Let me show you something real quick before you go. This is what happens to a family in your situation who didn't have this coverage when they needed it. Not to be dramatic — just so the decision you're making is an informed one."

That's not manipulation. That's information. The customer's decision should be made with full awareness of the stakes on both sides.

The EDET equivalent in insurance is the needs analysis. Before presenting any product, the professional has gathered:

- Current coverage (what they have and what's missing)
- Family situation and dependents
- Financial obligations and income replacement needs
- Budget for premium
- Prior claims or health history
- Timeline for decisions (any upcoming life changes?)

An insurance salesperson who leads with the product before understanding the need is presenting, not selling. The worksheet approach — systematically gathering information before structuring a recommendation — is exactly as applicable here as on an automotive floor.

Financial Services: The Commitment Process in Action

Financial advisors and planners deal constantly with the tension between client interest and client inertia. People know they should invest, they know they should have a financial plan, they know they should review their retirement accounts. They just don't do it.

The EDET principle here is about creating small commitments that lead to larger ones. The advisor who says "just let me run some quick numbers for you based on your current situation — no obligation, just so you have the information" is using the worksheet approach. Getting the client to share their financial information — income, current savings, risk tolerance, goals — is the commitment process in action.

Once someone has shared their financial picture with you, they are invested in what you're going to tell them. They want to hear the analysis. They want to know if they're on track. And the advisor who delivers that analysis competently and honestly has created the conditions for a transaction.

Time kills financial deals the same way it kills car deals. The client who says "let me get back to you after the holidays" is not coming back after the holidays unless you stay in front of them. Urgency in financial services is the cost of delay — inflation eroding savings, lost compounding, rising premiums as they age. These are real costs. Communicate them.

Home Services: The Written Estimate as the Worksheet

A contractor — kitchen remodeler, HVAC installer, roofing company, landscaper — has the same dynamics at play. A homeowner calls, you come out, you talk through what they want. The question is: do you go back to your truck and email them an estimate three days later, or do you sit at their kitchen table right now, pull out your worksheet, and build the scope of work together?

The one who builds it at the table closes at dramatically higher rates.

Here's why. When the estimate is built together, in real time, the homeowner has participated in creating it. They've made choices. They've said yes to certain options and no to others. They've invested thirty minutes in the process. They have ownership of the scope.

When the estimate arrives by email three days later, the homeowner opens it cold. They have no context for the numbers because they weren't part of building them. They shop it around. They get three other bids. The deal often dies.

Sit at the table. Build the worksheet together. Get a signature on the scope before you leave.

That's the EDET principle in home services. The worksheet is the scope document. Getting it signed — even as a preliminary agreement — is the commitment mechanism. Every day that passes between the site visit and the signed scope is a day the deal can die.

The Universal Human Psychology

All of these industry applications come back to the same foundation: human beings make purchase decisions emotionally, justify them logically, and are heavily influenced by process and commitment.

They feel better about decisions they've been guided through than ones they've arrived at alone and uncertain.

They trust professionals who seem organized and know the next step more than ones who seem to be making it up as they go.

They complete processes they've started more often than processes they haven't started, which is why getting someone to fill out any part of a worksheet — any part — is more valuable than leaving the sheet blank.

Time always creates space for doubt unless forward momentum fills it.

These are not automotive principles. These are human principles. Apply them wherever you sell.

One More Word for the Cross-Industry Reader

If you picked up this book because you're in real estate or insurance or financial planning and someone told you the automotive world had figured something out — you were told correctly.

Car dealerships close faster, with more structure, on higher tickets than almost any other retail environment. Not because car salespeople are smarter. Because the best dealerships have built and enforced process disciplines that other industries often let slide.

The EDET sheet and the Time Kills Deals urgency mindset are yours to adapt. Change the fields. Change the language. Keep the philosophy.

Get the information. Move forward every day. Run your process on every customer. Close more deals.

BOTTOM LINE: The two core principles of this book — urgency and consistent process — apply to every high-ticket sales environment. Human psychology doesn't change based on what's being sold. The worksheet concept, commitment psychology, and Time Kills Deals translate directly to real estate, insurance, financial services, home services, and beyond.

TAKEAWAYS:

- High-ticket sales in all industries involve the same emotional journey for buyers.
- In real estate, the buyer profile and pre-approval are the worksheet. Build them first.
- In insurance, create concrete urgency around the real cost of not deciding.
- In financial services, small financial disclosures are commitment psychology in action.
- In home services, build the scope at the table and get a signature before you leave.

PART THREE: BUILDING THE CULTURE

CHAPTER 13: BUILDING A CULTURE OF PROCESS

Individual talent is great. A salesperson who has internalized every principle in this book and runs the EDET process on every customer is a tremendous asset. They will be a consistent top performer. They will make good money and contribute meaningfully to the dealership's results.

But one great salesperson on a floor full of inconsistent ones cannot build a dealership. They can build a career.

If you're a manager or an owner reading this, the question is not just how to develop individual performers. The question is how to install process discipline as the cultural norm — so that every salesperson on your floor runs the process, every time, not because they're being watched, but because it's simply how business is done here.

Culture is the operating system that runs underneath all the individual performances. When the culture is strong, the floor produces predictably. When the culture is weak, results depend entirely on who had a good day and whether the right customers walked in.

This chapter is about installing the right culture.

The Foundation: Standards, Not Suggestions

The first and most important decision any sales manager makes about process is whether process requirements are standards or suggestions.

In dealerships where EDET is a standard, there is no deal brought to the desk without a completed sheet. Period. The manager sends the salesperson back if it's incomplete. After a few times, the salesperson learns. The behavior changes.

In dealerships where EDET is a suggestion, it gets used when convenient, skipped when uncomfortable, and ignored entirely by the veterans who have been there long enough to do things their own way. The results are inconsistent because the process is inconsistent.

You cannot build a process culture without establishing non-negotiable standards. Non-negotiable means consequences. It means consistency in enforcement. It means the same standard applies to the new hire and to the ten-year veteran.

This makes some managers uncomfortable, especially when the veteran in question produces decent numbers. The temptation is to carve out exceptions: *He's been here forever. He does things his own way. Leave him alone.*

Here is the problem with that exception: the floor watches everything. When the veteran gets to ignore the process, every newer salesperson files that away as evidence that the process is optional when you've been around long enough. The standard erodes. The culture weakens. The inconsistency spreads.

Standards only work when they apply to everyone. Including your best veteran. Especially your best veteran.

The Morning Huddle

The morning huddle — a ten-to-fifteen minute team meeting before the floor opens — is one of the most underused cultural tools in automotive sales.

Done right, the morning huddle accomplishes several things simultaneously:

- It sets the mindset for the day
- It reviews the previous day's performance against process standards
- It identifies customers who are coming back and ensures a plan is in place
- It reinforces specific skills through quick role-play
- It builds team accountability and energy

A typical morning huddle should include:

Numbers review: What did we close yesterday? What sheets were completed? What deals are in progress? (Two minutes)

Priority customers: Who are we expecting today? Is their follow-up confirmed? What do we know about their deal? (Three minutes)

Skill focus: One specific technique, one specific word track, one specific scenario. Something small and actionable that every salesperson can deploy today. (Five minutes)

Role-play: Spend two minutes doing a quick drill. Manager plays a skeptical customer; one salesperson works through the EDET introduction. Keep it brief, keep it sharp, keep it consistent. (Two to three minutes)

Energy: End with something that reminds people why they're here and what a great day looks like. Not a pep rally. A clear statement of expectations and belief.

Fifteen minutes. Every day. The cumulative effect of this daily discipline over a quarter is enormous.

Accountability Without Micromanagement

The word "accountability" makes some salespeople nervous because they associate it with surveillance. Being watched. Being second-guessed. Having a manager looking over their shoulder.

Real accountability is different. Real accountability is clear expectations, honest tracking, and regular honest conversations about performance against those expectations.

Here is a simple accountability structure for EDET process compliance:

Track the sheet completion rate. For every customer who enters the floor, how many result in a completed EDET sheet? This is not about forcing sheets on people who aren't remotely in a deal. This is about measuring whether the process is being run on the customers who qualify — the ones who expressed interest, looked at vehicles, went on a demo drive.

Review sheets in the evening. At the end of each day, a brief desk review of every sheet that came in. What was complete? What was missing? What needs follow-up tomorrow? This takes ten minutes and surfaces process gaps while they're still fresh.

Monthly process coaching. Every salesperson should have a monthly one-on-one with their manager — not just about numbers, but about process. What's working? What's not? Where are deals dying? Are the word tracks being used? Is there an area of the process they're avoiding?

The conversation about process is almost always more productive than the conversation about results, because process is what creates results. If the process is wrong, the results will be wrong. Fix the process, the results follow.

Installing Role-Play as a Practice Habit

Most salespeople resist role-play. It feels awkward. It feels fake. Nobody wants to simulate a sale with their manager or their peers when they've been "doing this for years."

Resistance to role-play is directly correlated with resistance to growth.

Every high-performing field that requires client communication uses deliberate practice. Lawyers moot. Surgeons simulate. Athletes drill fundamentals every single practice. The best salespeople in the world — in any industry — regularly practice their craft.

The resistance to role-play in sales often comes from ego. "I already know how to do this." The thing is — knowing how to do something and being able to execute it at the moment it matters, under pressure, with a real customer who is not cooperating — are very different things. Role-play builds the second skill.

Make role-play a regular part of your floor culture. Here's how:

Keep it short. A two-minute drill focused on one specific scenario is better than a thirty-minute marathon that exhausts everyone. The goal is repetition, not duration.

Take turns. Managers and salespeople both play customer and salesperson. Watching your manager handle the same scenario you just stumbled through is more instructive than any lecture.

Focus on the moments of friction. Don't role-play the easy parts. Role-play the worksheet introduction. Role-play the response to "I want to think about it." Role-play the T.O. Those are the moments that matter and the ones that need the most practice.

Make feedback specific and constructive. Not "that wasn't great." Instead: "The introduction was strong, but when she pushed back on the license, you backed off. Next time, here's exactly what you say: [specific word track]."

Over a quarter of consistent daily role-play, average salespeople become better-than-average salespeople. It is that simple.

Handling the Veteran Who Refuses to Use the Sheet

This is the most challenging management scenario in dealership process installation. The 10-year veteran who has been doing this their own way longer than some of their colleagues have been alive, who produces decent numbers, and who looks at the EDET process with barely concealed contempt.

Here's how the conversation usually goes when a manager first tries to enforce the standard:

Manager: "I need you to start using the sheet on every customer."

Veteran: "I don't need the sheet. I know how to read my customers. I've been doing this for ten years."

Manager: [backs off to avoid conflict]

That backing off is the death of the standard. And here's what happens next: the veteran notices. They tell their colleagues the sheet is optional. The colleagues don't use it. The floor's process discipline softens. The manager has just sacrificed the cultural standard to avoid one uncomfortable conversation.

Here is the better path.

First, have the conversation in private, with respect and without ultimatums. "I know you've been doing this a long time and you have real skills. I'm not questioning that. What I'm asking is that we run this process as a team standard, because the data shows deals that go through the full process close at a higher rate. You might be the exception — but I want us to find out with data."

Second, track the numbers. A veteran who actually is performing well without the sheet — whose closing rate and gross per deal are strong — is worth having a data-driven conversation with. Maybe there is something to learn from their approach. But most of the time, when you actually track the performance of the "I don't need the sheet" veterans, you find deals dying in places they can't fully account for. They're leaving money on the floor and don't know it.

Third, if the veteran refuses to comply with a direct standard after a professional conversation: you have a management decision to make about whether their performance justifies an exception to a rule that applies to everyone else. In most cases, it doesn't. And in many cases, once the veteran sees newer salespeople producing comparable numbers with the full process, the argument for "my way" gets harder to make.

Culture wins when standards are clear, consistent, and enforced with respect. Not rigidity. Respect and consistency.

The Manager's Role: Install, Reinforce, Model

The single most important thing a manager can do to build a process culture is to model the process themselves. When the manager walks through a demo T.O. and uses the EDET language. When the manager role-plays the worksheet introduction at the morning huddle. When the manager reviews the sheets at the end of the day and asks specific, process-focused questions.

The floor watches. Always. What the manager does consistently is what the floor treats as real. What the manager only talks about is what the floor ignores.

If you want a process culture: live the process yourself, in front of your team, every single day.

BOTTOM LINE: Culture is the operating system that determines whether individual training produces lasting results. Standards must apply to everyone. The morning huddle, daily accountability, regular role-play, and consistent management modeling are the tools that turn individual process knowledge into floor-wide culture.

TAKEAWAYS:

- Standards only work when they apply to everyone — especially the veteran who resists them.
- The morning huddle is fifteen minutes that compounds into massive results over a quarter.
- Track sheet completion rates. What gets measured gets done.
- Role-play builds the execution skill that knowledge alone never does.
- Managers who model the process build floors that run the process. This is non-negotiable.

CHAPTER 14: THE 30-DAY CHALLENGE

You've read the book. You've nodded along at the parts that made sense. You've recognized yourself in a few uncomfortable places. You understand the two keys and why they work.

Now comes the part that actually changes your results.

Everything in this book is meaningless unless you execute on it. Information without action is just entertainment. And in sales, entertainment doesn't pay the bills.

This chapter is your 30-day plan. It is structured for both individual salespeople and for managers installing these principles across a team. It is specific, it is actionable, and it requires nothing except the willingness to actually do it.

Here's the commitment: **30 days. No exceptions. Full process. Every customer.**

Not every customer where it feels comfortable. Every customer. Including the ones who look like tire kickers. Including the late Saturday appointment when you're exhausted. Including the customers where your instinct says "this one's not worth the full effort."

Especially those.

WEEK ONE: Foundation and Diagnosis

Goal: Understand exactly where you are and establish the habits that everything else depends on.

Day 1: Self-Audit

Before you do anything else, take an honest inventory. Review your last 30 days — not your numbers, your *process*. How often did you complete the EDET sheet? How often did you get the trade payoff before going to the desk? How often did you go to the desk with a specific payment target?

If you don't track these, you're estimating. Either way, be honest. The baseline you set today determines how you measure progress over the next 30 days.

Write down three specific process gaps — areas where you know you routinely skip a step, avoid a question, or take the easy road. These three gaps are your 30-day focus.

Days 2-3: Memorize the Master Word Track

Write out the master word track from Chapter 8 by hand. Multiple times. Then say it out loud. Ten times. Then in the mirror. Then to a colleague.

You are not memorizing it so you can recite it robotically. You are memorizing it so the structure is completely automatic and your conscious attention is free to focus on the customer. By Day 3, you should be able to deliver the worksheet introduction confidently, without hesitation, in your own natural voice.

Days 4-5: The Sheet, Every Customer

Starting today, the EDET sheet comes out on every customer who has identified a vehicle they're interested in. Not some of them. Every one.

Track the results. Not the closes — the *process*. Did you get the sheet out? Did the customer engage? What was their reaction? What did you learn?

Two things will happen this week. First, some customers will engage more readily than you expected. Your fear about "scaring them away" will start to look like the protection mechanism it actually is. Second, you will identify which specific part of the worksheet introduction feels awkward for you. That's the part you'll work on next week.

Days 6-7: Track and Reflect

At the end of Week One, review your notes. How many customers did you introduce the sheet to? What percentage engaged? Where did deals slow down? Which word tracks felt natural and which felt forced?

Write down one specific skill you want to improve in Week Two.

WEEK TWO: Skill Building and Practice

Goal: Improve execution quality and address the weak spots identified in Week One.

Day 8: Driver's License Practice

If asking for the driver's license is one of your weak points — and it is for many salespeople — spend time this day specifically on that moment. Write out your word track for introducing the license request. Practice it with a colleague. Practice it until the awkwardness is gone.

Remember: **customers don't get scared when you ask for information. They get scared when you don't know what you're doing.** Confidence in the ask comes from practice.

Days 9-10: The Payment Anchor

Spend two days with specific focus on getting the desired monthly payment before you go to the desk. Every customer. For the ones who say "I don't know," use the side-door technique from Chapter 8: ask what they're currently paying and whether they want to go higher, lower, or similar.

You should leave Week Two with the payment anchor feeling completely natural — because it is the most important piece of information you gather, and it should be second nature.

Days 11-12: The Trade Payoff

If getting the exact 10-day payoff has been something you defer, this is the week it becomes automatic. Every customer with a trade. Write out the conversation. Practice it. Do it every time.

The payoff conversation is not difficult. "Do you have your lender's app on your phone? Can you pull up the payoff real quick?" That's it. It is only uncomfortable if you've made it a big deal in your head.

Days 13-14: Role-Play Day

Set aside time on these days to role-play with a colleague or manager. Specifically:

- The EDET introduction
- The "I want to think about it" response

- The "just looking" engagement
- The T.O. introduction

Record yourself if possible. Watch it back. The things you notice about your own delivery — pacing, confidence, eye contact, word choice — are worth more than any external feedback.

WEEK THREE: Advanced Execution and Urgency Habits

Goal: Layer in the urgency principles and make the full process flow seamlessly from first contact to desk.

Days 15-16: The Urgency Audit

Review two or three deals from the past week where the customer left without buying. Trace them back through the interaction:

- At what point did forward momentum stop?
- Was there a moment of dead air that lasted too long?
- Was there a "let me know if you have any questions" that killed the momentum?

- Was there a point where you sensed hesitation and backed off instead of engaging it?

Identify your specific pattern of letting urgency die. This week, every time you sense a momentum drop, your job is to engage it rather than accommodate it.

Days 17-18: The Ten-Minute Rule

Practice the ten-minute rule this week: no customer goes more than ten minutes without a meaningful, forward-moving interaction. Set a mental timer. It will feel hyperactive at first. It will start to feel natural by the end of the week.

Days 19-20: Objection Response Rehearsal

Write out the five most common objections you face and your response to each. Not a general response — the specific word track that engages the real issue and moves the deal forward. Rehearse them. Specifically:

- "I want to think about it."
- "What's your best price?"
- "I need to talk to my spouse."
- "I'm not ready today, I'm just looking."

- "I was approved at my credit union at a better rate."

For each one: what is the real concern behind the objection? What question surfaces that concern? What do you say when you've surfaced it?

Days 21: Week Three Review

How many deals went to the desk with complete sheets this week? How did the urgency practice change the energy of your interactions? What's your one focus for Week Four?

WEEK FOUR: Consistency, Measurement, and the Long Game

Goal: Lock in the habits, measure the results, and build the mindset for permanent performance.

Days 22-24: Full Process, Full Focus

By now, the process should be feeling significantly more natural than it did at the start. This week, the focus is consistency — not getting better at individual steps but running the full sequence seamlessly.

Think of it as practice runs for the permanent version of your professional self. You are not trying the process anymore. You are *running* it.

Day 25: The "Be Back" Recovery

Identify every customer who left without buying in the past 30 days and build a structured follow-up plan for anyone you haven't fully closed the loop with. For each one:

- What specifically prevented the deal from closing?
- What would need to change for them to come back and buy?
- What is your specific re-engagement approach?

A good follow-up is not "just checking in to see if you made a decision." A good follow-up has new information, answers a question they had, or surfaces a specific reason to act now. "I wanted to let you know the color you were interested in just came in." "Our current rate special ends this weekend." Specific. Relevant. Action-oriented.

Days 26-27: Manager Integration (For Managers Reading This)

If you're a manager, this week you review your team's process compliance data and have individual conversations with each salesperson. Not about numbers — about process. What are they doing well? Where are they still avoiding the uncomfortable steps? What coaching does each person need going into Month Two?

For individual salespeople: find a manager or mentor and have a frank conversation about your 30-day progress. Ask for specific feedback on your worksheet process and your urgency habits.

Days 28-30: Measurement and Commitment

Pull your numbers for the past 30 days and compare them to your baseline from Day 1. Look specifically at:

- Sheet completion rate
- Closing rate (deals closed / customers who identified a vehicle)
- Gross per deal
- "Be-backs" who returned and bought

Compare these to the prior period. In most cases — not all, but most — salespeople who committed fully to this 30-day process see measurable improvement in at least two of these metrics within the first month. The improvement compounds over time.

Write a commitment for Month Two. Be specific: what process habits are you locking in permanently? What areas need continued focus? What does your best professional self look like at the six-month mark?

For Managers: Rolling This Out to a Team

If you're installing these principles across a team, the 30-day structure looks slightly different.

Week One: Team introduction. Morning huddle setup. Establish baseline metrics. Individual conversations about the EDET standard.

Week Two: Daily skills focus in morning huddles. First round of individual coaching conversations. Establish the rule: no sheet, no desk.

Week Three: Role-play becomes a daily practice. Review actual sheets for quality. Begin tracking completion rates. Identify your highest-compliance salespeople and leverage them as informal coaches.

Week Four: Performance review against baseline. Recognize public wins. Address ongoing resistance individually and privately. Commit to the standards for Month Two.

The critical thing: momentum. Don't let a week pass without reinforcing the standards. Don't let a deal go to the desk without a sheet. Don't let the morning huddle slide because things got busy. This is the month the culture gets built. Don't waste it.

The Daily Habits That Make This Permanent

Beyond the 30-day plan, certain daily habits make process discipline self-sustaining:

Write your number on the board every day. Not your results. Your process metrics. How many sheets did you complete? How many payoffs did you get? How many payment targets did you anchor? Numbers make habits visible, and visible habits are easier to maintain.

Review one deal every evening. Just one. What went right? What went wrong? What was the specific moment where the momentum changed? This daily practice — five minutes at the end of each day — accelerates development faster than almost anything else.

Say the word tracks out loud before you walk the floor. Not to anyone in particular. Just out loud, in the parking lot or the break room. The physical act of speaking the words makes them more automatic. Your mouth learns the path; your conscious mind doesn't have to navigate it every time.

Find one person to be accountable to. A colleague, a manager, a peer. Someone who knows your goals and checks in. Accountability does not require surveillance. It just requires one other person who cares whether you did what you said you were going to do.

BOTTOM LINE: The 30-day challenge is where the book stops being information and starts being transformation. Every day, full process, no exceptions. Track it. Measure it. Review it. Build the habits that make this automatic. The salesperson who completes this challenge honestly will not sell the same way in Month Two that they sold in Month One.

TAKEAWAYS:

- Week One: diagnose your gaps and establish basic habits.
- Week Two: build specific skills on the weak points you identified.
- Week Three: layer in urgency habits and objection responses.
- Week Four: measure results and commit to the permanent version.
- Daily habits — tracking, reviewing, speaking the word tracks — make process discipline self-sustaining.

BACK MATTER

CONCLUSION: TIME KILLS DEALS. EVERY DEAL. EVERY TIME.

We started with two keys. Let's end there.

Time Kills Deals.

Every minute a customer is not moving forward, they are moving backward. The emotional energy that drives purchase decisions is perishable. Doubt, the internet, competitors, and family members with opinions are all waiting for you to slow down and give them an opening. Don't give them the opening. Keep it moving. Always keep it moving.

Every Deal Every Time.

Full process. Every customer. No exceptions, no pre-judgments, no coasting on easy customers while the hard ones walk out the door. The worksheet is your closing weapon — not paperwork, not administrative burden, but the single most powerful tool you have for converting a shopper into a buyer. Use it on everyone. Every time.

Here is what I want to leave you with.

The best salespeople are not the most charming. They're not the loudest or the smoothest or the ones with the best stories. The best salespeople are the most disciplined. The ones who decide, at some point in their career, that they are going to run the process all the way through, every single time, regardless of how they feel that day or how the customer is presenting.

That decision — to stop being selective, to stop coasting, to stop letting discomfort be an excuse — is the decision that separates average from great.

Nobody woke up a top performer. They built it. One deal at a time. One worksheet at a time. One uncomfortable conversation at a time. One morning huddle and one role-play and one "let me just see what the numbers look like for you" at a time.

You now have everything you need.

The principles are clear. The psychology is explained. The word tracks are written out. The 30-day plan is in front of you.

Two keys. Zero excuses.

Get to work.

THE EVERY DEAL EVERY TIME WORKSHEET

(Reproducible — Make Copies for Daily Use)

```

---

---

EVERY DEAL EVERY TIME WORKSHEET

Dr. Chris Guam Santos — Every Deal Every Time

---

---

DATE: ____________________ SALESPERSON:

________________________

---

---

CUSTOMER INFORMATION
```

Customer Name (Full):

Phone Number:

[ ] Driver's License / ID Photo Obtained

Address (from License):

VEHICLE OF INTEREST

Year / Make / Model:

Stock Number:

Color:

____

____

FINANCIAL INFORMATION

____

____

Money Down:

$__________________________________

Desired Monthly Payment:

$________________________________

Preferred Term: __________ months

Outside Lender (if pre-approved):

____

Outside Approval Rate: _________% Term: ________ months

____

____

TRADE-IN INFORMATION

____

____

Trade Year / Make / Model:

____

Trade Mileage:

____

[ ] Trade Photos Obtained

Trade Lender / Bank (exact name):

____

Exact 10-Day Payoff:

$____

Payoff Good Through (date):

____

____

____

CUSTOMER COMMITMENT STATUS

____

____

Please Circle One:

REAL CUSTOMER — READY TO PURCHASE TODAY

JUST THINKING – NEED TO LOOK AT OTHER VEHICLES

____

____

NOTES / ADDITIONAL INFORMATION:

____

____

MANAGER RULE: If this sheet is not filled out, we do not have

a deal. Return to the floor and complete before

presenting to the desk.

==

==

```
```

QUICK REFERENCE: SCRIPTS & WORD TRACKS

The Master EDET Introduction

> *"I don't want to waste your time or mine going back and forth. If you like the vehicle, the next step is we just put everything on one sheet and see if the numbers make sense for you. Takes about three minutes and it'll tell us whether we're in the right range."*

Alternative Introduction

> *"The way we make this easy is we put everything on one sheet so we can see if the numbers work for you. If they do,

> *great. If they don't, no problem. But this will save you a lot of time."**

By Customer Type

First-Time Buyer:

> *"What we're going to do is make this as straightforward as possible. Once you find a vehicle you like, we're going to sit down and put everything on one sheet together — your payment goal, what you're putting down, all of it — so you can see exactly what you're looking at before any decisions are made. Nothing happens without you knowing the full picture first."*

Skeptical Customer:

> *"Instead of playing the pricing game, let me show you something different. We're going to put everything on one sheet

> *right now — your trade, your payment target, your down payment — and I'll show you exactly where we land. No back and forth. No mystery numbers. You'll see the full picture up front."**

Trade-In Customer:

> *"Absolutely, we're going to get that figured out for you. What I need from you is a quick look at the vehicle and your exact 10-day payoff. While you pull that up, let me get some photos and the mileage, and we'll have everything ready so your trade is already factored in when we sit down."**

"Just Looking" Customer:

> *"No problem at all. What kind of vehicle are you looking for? I'll show you what we have."**

> *[After demo drive:] *"I know you said you were just looking — but you looked like you enjoyed that one. Is it more the timing, the payment, or something about the vehicle that's holding you back?"**

Payment-Sensitive Customer:

> **"Let's make sure we hit that for you. Let me grab your down payment, payoff on your current vehicle, and whether you have financing already in place. Once I have that, I can tell you quickly whether we can hit your number."**

Handling Objections

"I want to think about it."

> **"Completely understand. What part would you like to think about? Is it the payment, the trade, or something about the vehicle itself?"**

"What's your best price?"

> *"I appreciate you asking it that way — here's what I'd rather do: let's put everything together on one sheet so you're seeing the full picture. Price, trade, payment — all in one place. That way you know exactly what you're getting, not just one piece of the puzzle."*

"I need to talk to my spouse."

> *"Of course. Before you do — let me put the actual numbers together so you have something concrete to show them. A real number is a lot more useful than 'we talked about it.' Takes five minutes. Want to do that now?"*

"I'm not ready today."

> *"That's totally fine. Can I ask — what would need to happen for you to be ready? Is there a timing thing, or is it

> *more about getting comfortable with the numbers?"**

"I was pre-approved at my credit union."

> *"That's great — let me know the rate and term, because sometimes we can match it or do better through our lenders. Either way, I want you to have the best rate available."*

Customer won't provide driver's license:

> *"Completely understand. I just need it to verify your information and keep things moving — same as any financial transaction. I'll take a quick photo and hand it right back."*

Customer doesn't know payment target:

> *"What are you paying on your current vehicle?" [They answer.] "And would you like to go higher, lower, or about the same?"*

Phrases to Eliminate Permanently

✖ "Let me know if you have any questions."

✖ "Take all the time you need."

✖ "They said they'll come back this weekend."

✖ "This one probably isn't serious."

✖ "I don't want to push too hard."

Phrases to Use Every Day

✓ "Let's see if the numbers make sense for you."

✓ "What do you think — did it feel like the right fit?"

✓ "I want to make sure we have everything ready before I go to the desk."

✓ "Let me show you while we're here..."

✓ "Before you go, let me put the actual numbers together so you have something real."

✓ "What would need to be true for you to feel comfortable moving forward today?"

ABOUT THE AUTHOR

Dr. Chris Guam Santos is a Chamorro American Pacific Islander, native of Guam, and 10-year resident of Richmond, Virginia. He is a sales performance expert, dealership trainer, and one of the most direct voices in automotive sales development today.

Dr. Santos has held every major role on the dealership floor — salesperson, closer, finance manager, desk manager, general sales manager, and General Manager — giving him a ground-level perspective that no outside trainer can replicate. He developed and refined the *Every Deal Every Time* framework during his time as General Manager at Hyman Bros Automotive and General Sales Manager at CMA Kia. His two master keys — **Time Kills Deals** and **Every Deal Every Time** — have transformed floors, rebuilt cultures, and turned struggling salespeople into consistent producers.

Beyond the automotive world, Dr. Santos has applied these frameworks to real estate, insurance, financial services, and high-ticket B2B sales, proving that the psychology of urgency and commitment is universal.

A proud Chamorro American Pacific Islander and one of the few in the automotive industry to rise to the General Manager level in Virginia, Dr. Santos brings a perspective shaped not just by experience, but by the resilience required to build authority in spaces where people who look like him rarely hold the chair.

Beyond the dealership floor, Dr. Santos is a recognized cultural figure in both the automotive and arts communities. He was named Guam's first-ever Best Hip Hop Artist by the Guam Legislature at Guam's inaugural Island Music Awards — a formal commendation signed and sealed by the 30th Legislature of Guam in Hagåtña. He is a charter member of the William and Mary Hip Hop Collection at the Special Collections department of the College of William and Mary — the most comprehensive archive of Virginia hip-hop culture in existence. He serves as an officer of the CNMI Society of America and a member of the Guam Society of America, both based in Washington, D.C.

Dr. Chris Guam Santos is available for speaking engagements, dealership training programs, and sales consulting at www.ChrisGuamSantos.com.

This book is dedicated to every dealership, every floor, every team that is willing to commit to the process. Two keys. Zero excuses.

END OF MANUSCRIPT

Time Kills Deals: Are You the Time Killer? — Book 1 of The Keys Series

By Dr. Chris Guam Santos | Santos Performance Group